Introduc

The historic market town of Holywell †
Winefride's Holy Well, whose reputed
grims here for centuries, earning it a reputa......... .. ....
town lies among undulating countryside overlooking the Dee Estuary, and at
the top of the wooded Greenfield Valley, now a Heritage Park. The valley contains various ancient monuments, including the 8thC Wat's Dyke and 12thC
Basingwerk Abbey, as well as the remains of mills and factories that made
the valley a major industrial centre in the 18thC. Near Holywell are attractive
villages, including Whitford, the home of Thomas Pennnant, the renowned
18thC naturalist, traveller and writer.

South of Holywell is Halkyn Mountain, part of Halkyn Common, an
ancient urban common, covering nearly 2000 acres of mainly grassland
grazed by sheep. Mostly owned by the Grosvenor Estate, it is a narrow upland
plateau of carboniferous limestone, with its highest point being Moel y Gaer
Iron-Age hillfort (994 feet). Scattered settlements lie within a landscape of
capped shafts and old workings – a legacy of its intensive exploitation for
lead and quarrying for limestone, chert, clay, sand and gravel. Lead-mining
began with the Romans and ceased in the 1980s. During the 18th and 19th
centuries Halkyn Mountain became a major lead producer, with large scale
deep mines replacing shallow workings.

Its designation as an Open Access area and its network of paths used by
miners and commoners provide a great opportunity to explore this wonderful
open upland landscape – but take care near old workings.

The 20 circular walks in this book explore the area's delightful contrast-
ing countryside, providing a great insight into its social and industrial history. They link villages with traditional country inns and visit many places of
interest. Most are accessible by bus.

The routes, which range from 2 to 7 miles, follow public rights of way or
permissive paths, and cross Open Access land. A key feature is that individ-
ual routes, as well as containing shorter walk options, can easily be linked to
provide longer day walks, if required. Walking boots are recommended, along
with appropriate clothing to protect against the elements. Please remember
that the condition of paths can vary according to season and weather. Contact
Flintshire Highways Department regarding any problems encountered.

Each walk has a detailed map and description which enables the route to
be followed without difficulty, but be aware that changes in detail can occur
at any time. The location of each walk is shown on the back cover and a sum-
mary of their key features is also given. This includes an estimated walking
time, but allow more time to enjoy the scenery. Please observe the country
code. *Enjoy your walking!*

GREENFIELD VALLEY

DESCRIPTION A fascinating 3 mile walk exploring the narrow steep-sided wooded Greenfield Valley, now a Heritage Park, containing mill-ponds, sites of industrial archaeological interest, farm museum, Visitor Centre and café. Scheduled Ancient Monuments include 8thC Wat's Dyke, 12thC Basingwerk Abbey and the famous St Winefride's Well. The valley also contains the remains of the steepest conventional passenger railway in Great Britain and the popular Royal Oak pub midway. Allow 2–4 hours for there is much to see and enjoy.

START Greenfield Valley A548 car park [SJ 197775] or Holywell High Street [SJ 185759]

DIRECTIONS From Holywell take the B5121 down to Greenfield. Turn right along the A548 towards Flint. The Greenfield Valley car park is on the right.

The Greenfield Valley, near to sources of lead and other ores, and with easy access by sea to Liverpool, developed rapidly during the 18thC as an important industrial centre, regarded as the cradle of the Industrial Revolution in North Wales. Its constant flow of water – 4,000 gallons a minute – which never froze, provided the power for a line of mills and factories that stretched down the narrow valley. It steadily declined during the 19thC with the development of steam power, and the need for larger sites and better port facilities.

I From an information board at the car park corner enter the Heritage Park. Follow the pathway round the perimeter of.Basingwerk Abbey (**A**). *Founded in 1132, it became an important centre for monks of the Cistercian Order until its dissolution by Henry VIII in 1536. They established corn and fulling mills, and created a cultural community, which became the home of many Welsh poets.* After passing the Visitor Centre (**B**), with a cafe nearby, turn LEFT past a former school and the side of the Farm Museum (**C**)

to reach the bend of a lane. *Just to the west is a mill pool (**D**) all that remains of the important Parys Mine Company copper works, built in 1787 by Thomas Williams, known as 'The Copper King' for his success in producing copper bolts, rudder fittings and sheathing for wooden sailing ships.* Go up the lane signposted to various sites, soon passing the former Abbey Wire Mill (**E**) – *which made copper and brass wire* – and its mill pond. Go past the Lower Cotton Mill (**F**) – *once an impressive six storey building, powered by an 18ft high water wheel, used for spinning cotton brought from the Americas between 1785-1840. Later it was used by a miller/ flour dealer.* Continue by the Flour Mill pool.

2 As the lane begins to rise, follow a waymarked path close to the lake edge, soon passing to the right of large iron gates and on through the site of Meadow Mill (**G**) – *which made rollers for printing patterns on cloth and copper sheets.* Cross the mill pool outlet and dam and go through a car park to its entrance at Bryn Celyn. Go through a kissing gate by a barrier and along a track past a former brick clock tower down to large gates at a fenced off site. Turn LEFT along a path by the tall fence then up through trees to a waymarked path junction and bend RIGHT up to join the former railway line near a descending path. Follow it RIGHT up the wooded valley. Soon take a waymarked path on the right down through trees to a rectangular brick chimney and go across the dam of Battery Pool adjoining the former Greenfield Mills site (**H**). *Established in 1776, the Battery Works produced brass pots and pans, which were sent via Liverpool to Africa and exchanged for slaves.*

3 Turn LEFT along the pool's western side, then take the path's right fork to the Royal Oak (**I**). Turn LEFT down the car park to a stream, then go up a stepped path through the trees. At its top, turn RIGHT along the lower path, soon alongside a wall and past a chimney to a kissing gate. Follow the path down to the B5121. Turn LEFT past the site of Holywell Textile Mill (**J**) – *established in 1883 as the Welsh Flannel Manufacturing Company. The water was* *excellent for textile finishing processes. It closed in 1986.*

4 Continue to the entrance of St Winefride's Well (**K**) (*open daily 10.00–16.00*). *The legend of the miracle-working spring begins in 660 AD, when Winefride, a young girl, rejected the advances of Caradog, a local chieftain. In his anger, he cut off her head. Where it came to rest, a spring began to flow from the ground. Miraculously, she was restored to life by her uncle*

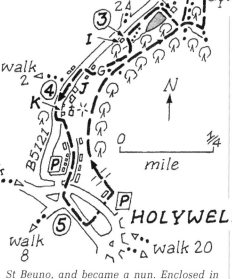

Greenfield

walk 2

to Flint

Bryn Celyn

walk 2A

walk 3

walk 2

P

dyke

N

0   ¼
mile

HOLYWELL

walk 8   walk 20

LEFT through a gateway to St James church. *When an earlier church was rebuilt in 1770, it was dedicated to St James, reputedly in reaction to superstitious practices at the Well. Because the valley muffled the church bell, a man would walk through the streets ringing a small bell, known as the 'Walking Steeple'.* Behind the church is the Holywell Castle mound. Bear RIGHT past its congested hillside graveyard and on up Well Street. Cross the inner ring road to reach Holywell centre.

5 Walk up the High Street. and just past the Red Lion, turn LEFT along Tower Gardens. At its end descend steps, go through the underpass and along the left-hand side of the car park. After the pelican crossing follow the pathway down into Greenfield Valley. Go under the arched bridge passing the site of Holywell station. *Built in 1869 to serve local quarries, the standard gauge branch line provided a passenger service from Greenfield until 1954. The 'Little Train' as it was known steamed up a gradient of 1 in 27.* Follow the former railway track down the wooded valley, shortly passing close to your outward route, then later briefly joining it. Just beyond the path rising back on your right by a side valley take another path heading up the wooded slope (or simply continue down the track) to reach a level path by the wood edge. Follow it LEFT – *shortly passing the embanked remains of Wat's Dyke on your right.* Follow the path down to rejoin the old railway track. Eventually the track narrows and crosses a footbridge. Soon afterwards the path does a U-turn down to join your outward route.

St Beuno, and became a nun. Enclosed in an early 16thC chapel, the famous well chamber, with bath, renowned for its healing properties, has attracted pilgrims for many centuries, including Henry V in 1416 and James II, who visited in 1686 to pray for a son. It was once littered with the crutches of the cured. In 1917, the well suddenly went dry, after men working on the Milwr Tunnel breached its source. Jobs were lost in the valley, the community was outraged, and it was 9 months before an alternative source was found! Continue up the road to turn

GREENFIELD DOCK

DESCRIPTION A 6 mile (**A**) or 5 mile (**B**) walk of great variety and interest from a once thriving industrial valley to the former port which served it. The route passes through Greenfield Heritage Park, then later an upland farm before descending in stages, enjoying extensive views, to Llanerch-y-mor, with its 17thC inn and Abakhan Fabrics Craft and Mill Shop, both offering refreshment options. After passing the entombed ship, the Duke of Lancaster, it follows the coastal path to Greenfield Dock. Allow about 3½ hours, but more for enjoying the many sights. An alternative 4¼ mile walk (**C**) is included. The route can be started at point 4 near St Winefride's Well entrance (car park nearby) or joined here from Holywell centre, if you prefer a lingering finish in the Heritage Park
START Greenfield Valley A548 car park [SJ 197775].
DIRECTIONS See **Walk 1**.

*G*reenfield Dock *was once a busy port in the 18th and 19th centuries, with up to 40 ships trading in raw materials and finished products from industries in the Greenfield Valley. In 1802, a sailing ship ferry service between Greenfield-Parkgate-Chester was established. Between 1857-1865, the iron ship 'Fanny' provided a 1½ hour passenger service to Liverpool. In the 1870s two other similar services were short lived. Shifting channels in the Dee Estuary meant that increasingly only small boats had access to the port, and along with local industries, its importance steadily declined. Nothing remains of the large wharf built in the 18thC, but small fishing boats still use the narrow inlet.*

1 Follow sections 1 and 2 of **Walk 1**.

3 For **Walk A**, continue with section 3 of **Walk 1**. (For **Walk C**, cross the B5121 to go up nearby Bryn Celyn/Spring Bank no through road. At a junction keep ahead, and

just beyond Oakmere House take a signposted path ahead, soon enclosed and passing houses, to enter a field at point **5**)

4 Just before the former mill showroom, with the entrance to St Winefride's Well beyond, cross to the small car park and track opposite. Follow the track along the Gowdal valley, soon passing the gated entrance to the Holywell Level lead mine (1773-1906). *Boats, moved by men pushing against the walls, were used to carry miners and transport ore, and in the late 18thC, 'tourist' boats trips along the level were popular. By 1830, a tramway had replaced the boats.* Continue along the track, later bending RIGHT towards a cattle-grid. Immediately before it, bear LEFT to continue beside the fence and on through a wet area of shrub to reach a kissing gate. Keep ahead by the fence later passing a children's' play area to reach a gate onto a lane. Follow it RIGHT up to Moor Farm. Go along the edge of the farmyard, past a mast and over two stiles. Continue along a farm track to a stile, then down the edge of two fields – *enjoying views across the Dee estuary to the Wirral and Liverpool* – to reach a field corner by houses. Here, turn sharp LEFT.

5 Go across the field and through a way-marked gap in the tree boundary ahead. Continue across the next field to a stile in its recessed corner, then to another stile ahead. Now angle away from the fence across the field's upper slope to cross a stile midway in the hedge ahead by a large tree. Go along the field edge to a stile in the corner, then along a hedge-lined green track. When it bends right towards Stokyn Hall, cross a stile ahead. Descend the field to a stile below into a small wooded valley, then follow the path down to cross a footbridge over the Afon Marsiandwr. *Upstream is a small waterfall.* Follow the path up to a stile and up a field to another stile onto a lane. Follow it RIGHT. (For **Walk B**, follow the lane down to the A548. Cross the stile opposite and continue to the railway line. Cross with care, then follow the embankment to join the coastal path.)

6 On the first bend, take a signposted path over a stile on the left and go across

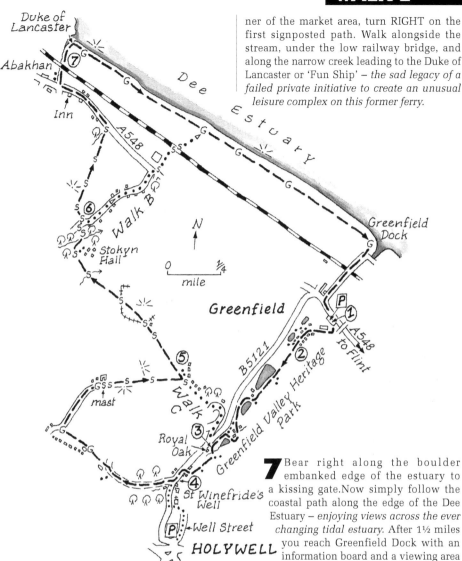

ner of the market area, turn RIGHT on the first signposted path. Walk alongside the stream, under the low railway bridge, and along the narrow creek leading to the Duke of Lancaster or 'Fun Ship' – *the sad legacy of a failed private initiative to create an unusual leisure complex on this former ferry.*

7 Bear right along the boulder embanked edge of the estuary to a kissing gate. Now simply follow the coastal path along the edge of the Dee Estuary – *enjoying views across the ever changing tidal estuary.* After 1½ miles you reach Greenfield Dock with an information board and a viewing area overlooking the estuary. *It is hard to imagine that this narrow creek was once a bustling port.* Follow Dock Road to the A548 at Greenfield. *As you cross the railway line, note the elegant former Holywell Junction Station, built in 1847-8 of Italianate brick and stone, and closed in the 1960s.* Turn LEFT back to the Heritage Park car park.

the field to cross a stile by a telegraph pole – *offering a good view of Mostyn Docks.* Go down the field, past a waymarked telegraph post to a stile below. Follow the waymarked path across two further fields and down through trees to the A548. Follow the pavement opposite to reach The Old Tavern Inn. Continue along the road, perhaps to visit the cafe at Abakhan – *a former 18thC lead-smelting works.* Otherwise, at the cor-

GORSEDD ROUND

DESCRIPTION A choice of 5½ mile (**A**), 5 mile (**B**) or 2½ mile (**C**) walks linking the villages of Gorsedd, Carmel and Pantasaph with the attractive undulating countryside to the north, using field paths, bridleways and quiet lanes. Allow about 3½ hours. The route includes the option of a shorter direct return to Gorsedd as shown.

START Crossroads by the Druid Inn, Gorsedd [SJ 153767].

DIRECTIONS Gorsedd lies west of Holywell, signposted off the A5026.

*G*orsedd *area has been occupied by man since pre-historic times, evidenced by the two Bronze Age burial mounds at the western end of the village, which were later associated with the Druids. The Druid Inn, possibly dating from the 12thC, and the oldest building in the village, stands at the crossroads of two ancient highways – the Chester to Caernarvon turnpike coach road, and the toll road from the coast. St. Paul's church was built in 1852, along with one in Brynford, from public subscription, in response to the controversial decision to dedicate the new planned Protestant church at Pantasaph as Roman Catholic. The nearby Church Hall was built at the same time, and served as the village school until 1953.*

1 Go down the road signposted to Whitford, over the A5026, and on down past 17thC Waen farm – to reach crossroads by The Old Toll Cottage – *where tolls were once taken for animals, coal, and limestone.* Continue ahead (Downing), then turn RIGHT along a side road. Just before 16thC Mertyn Abbot, take a signposted path over a stile on the left. ((For **Walk C** continue past Mertyn Abbot to join the return route at the junction.) Go across the field to a stile, then along the edge of the next large field. After a stile follow the field/wood edge above a stream to a stile in the corner. Follow the path down

through trees to cross a stream and a stile beyond. Go up the field edge to cross a stile in the corner. Keep ahead to cross a fence and an iron ladder-stile in the next field corner. Follow the path alongside the large perimeter fence of a nearby house to another iron ladder-stile, and continue via two stiles to a road.

2 Follow it RIGHT. *Visible to your left are the 18thC stables of the former Downing Hall, home of Thomas Pennant (see* **Walk 4***).* Go past Downing Boarding Kennels then The Tower – *a castellated gothic folly tower built in 1810, now a private house.* Follow the road down to a junction by Lower Lodge and keep ahead to reach the entrance to Forest Hill trout farm. If you're not tempted to feed the fish or enjoy tea and coffee, continue up the road and past appropriately named River View. Shortly, turn RIGHT up Mertyn Downing Lane on a signposted bridleway. After passing houses continue up a track.

3 When the track splits you have a choice. (For **Walk B**, take the right fork and follow it up the hillside. When it bends left, go half-right to follow a hedge-lined bridleway to Bryn Teg. The bridleway continues along its access track. At a track junction, turn left and follow it to a road by Pen-y-Palmant. Turn RIGHT and resume text at point **4**.) For **Walk A** take the LEFT fork towards Kennels Farm. Keep ahead to pass between dwellings. After a gate follow a track to cross a stile ahead. *Pause to take in the views across the estuary to the Wirral. Prominent is the entombed Duke of Lancaster ship.* Go along the field edge and over a stile in the corner. Turn LEFT, then RIGHT in the field corner and follow the fence to a stile in the far corner onto a track by Mertyn Isaf. Turn RIGHT up the track, passing Mertyn Crewe to join a lane. Follow it past cottages to a junction by Groesffordd. Keep ahead along Llwyn Ifor Lane soon joining **Walk B** at Pen-y-Palmant.

4 Follow the road to a junction by Mertyn Abbott and turn LEFT. Follow the road past Mertyn Uchaf and up to a junction. Turn RIGHT and cross a stile on the left. Keep ahead up the edge of the field, then cross a farm track. Keep ahead. Just beyond the end of the short holly boundary you have a choice. (For a direct return to Gorsedd continue ahead to the left of a line of trees to a stile by a small ruin. Follow a green track to the A5026, then the road opposite back to Gorsedd.) For the main route, bear LEFT to cross a nearby stream and stile, then go up the field to a stile to reach the A5026. Take the signposted path opposite up the edge of a field, soon bending LEFT past houses to cross a stile after about 20 yards. Follow the narrow path between houses to a road, then take the signposted path opposite to reach a higher road on the outskirts of Carmel. Turn RIGHT and go up Ffordd Ddreiniog on a path signposted to Pantasaph.

5 At its end cross a stile and continue along the field edge. At the boundary corner keep ahead up the field to follow telegraph poles to a stile, then follow a path up to a road. Continue down the road into Pantasaph – *soon with the Friary to your left (for information see* **Walk 8***).* At the junction, turn RIGHT along Monastery Road past the former Fielding Arms Hotel. After passing the last of a line of houses, cross a waymarked stile on the right just beyond a gate. Go across the field towards red-bricked houses, passing close to a telegraph pole, and on to cross a

stile. Go up the field, over a stile and along a path between houses to an estate road. Follow it LEFT to join a road near the start.

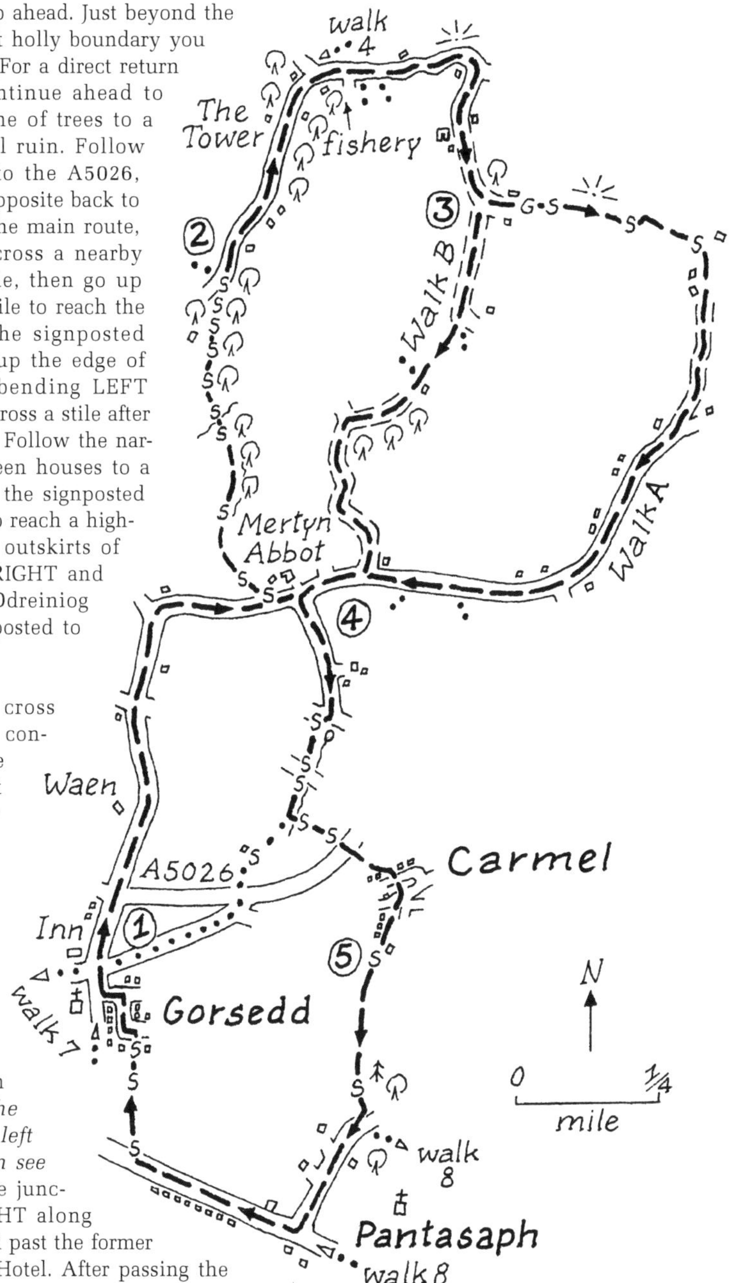

Map labels: walk 4, The Tower, fishery, walk B, walk A, ② ③ ④ ⑤ ①, Mertyn Abbot, Waen, A5026, Carmel, Inn, Gorsedd, N, 0 — ¼ mile, walk 8, Pantasaph, walk 8

WHITFORD WOOD & DOWNING

DESCRIPTION A 4 mile (**A**) walk passing through part of the Mostyn Estate and the adjoining former Downing estate. The route features attractive woodland and the ruin of Downing Hall, once the home of Thomas Pennant, the renowned 18thC naturalist, traveller and writer. Allow about 2½ hours for the full route. Alternative 2½ mile (**B**) or 2¼ mile (**C**) walks are included.
START Whitford [SJ 147782] or Maes Pennant [SJ 161798].
DIRECTIONS Whiford lies west of Holywell and is signposted off the A5026. Park tidily in the village centre near the church.

*W*hitford *is a small attractive village of some antiquity. A church, believed to date from the 7thC, was recorded here in the Doomsday Book. The present church of St Beuno and St Mary, with its two 17thC entrance gates, dates from the early 16thC. It contains some interesting artefacts. Its clock face is dated 1843. Nearby is the 17thC Huntsman Inn, formerly the Mostyn Arms. Whitford is associated with two renowned families, whose estates adjoined – the Mostyns, from Mostyn Hall, and the Pennants, notably Thomas Pennant (1726-98), who was born and lived at the nearby family home of Downing Hall. He received many honours and acclaim for his books on zoology and his extensive journeys in Britain and Europe. His book on The history of the Parishes of Whiteford and Holywell, published in 1776, provides a fascinating insight into the area. His unmarked grave is inside the church, whilst, that of his self-taught illustrator, Moses Griffiths, is on the northeast side of the graveyard.*

I Just beyond the village school entrance at information boards and a plaque commemorating Thomas Pennant take the signposted bridleway between the school and the rear of houses to a stile/bridle gate. Go half-

LEFT across the large field towards a distant lodge. At a bridle gate in the fence ahead, turn RIGHT and follow the waymarked path by the fence to go through a bridle gate in the corner, and another further ahead. (For **Walk C**, turn right along the tree-lined field edge, through a bridle gate and on along a track. Go past Coed Isa farm and down its driveway to a road. Follow it right down to point **4** just before Lower Lodge.) Keep ahead on the waymarked bridleway to join a waymarked fence corner – *with a view west to the watchtower on Coed y Garreg*. Continue beside the fence – *enjoying views across the Dee Estuary*. At its corner near the lodge go across the field to a bridle gate into Whitford Wood.

2 Shortly at a waymarked bridleway/path junction you have another choice. (For **Walk B** follow the path along the wood edge. At a waymarked path junction take the left fork. After about 100 yards at a path junction keep ahead to descend into a side valley. Follow the path past a waymarker post, over a sleeper bridge then by the stream past a large footbridge to a road. Follow it right down to point **4** just before Lower Lodge.) For **Walk A** follow the bridleway through the wood to a bridle gate and on across a field to reach a road by Rhewl-Mostyn. Make a short diversion to the nearby T-junction. *Nearby is Drybridge Lodge. Built in 1849 this two-storeyed castellated lodge not only has the public road passing underneath it, but also the former horse and carriage drive from Mostyn Hall to Whitford passing through it.* Return and continue along the road. After passing signposted paths, take a signposted bridleway on the left at the wood end. Follow it down into the narrow wooded valley to join a path above the stream, with a large footbridge to the left. Follow the path east through the valley to a path junction by a telegraph pole with a lamp. Here turn RIGHT and follow the path to Ffordd Ysgubor in Maes Pennant. Turn RIGHT, then angle LEFT along a pathway to cross another road.

3 Continue through Maes Pennant past the school, church, shops, a surgery, and police station. At a minor road at the far end of a wood, do a U-turn to go through a

8

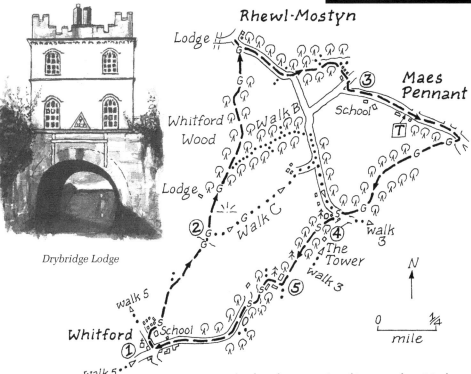

Rhewl·Mostyn

Drybridge Lodge

nearby small gateway. *The next section follows the old route to Downing Hall through surprisingly unspoilt countryside, later with the ruin of Thomas Pennant's mill among the trees to your left.* Keep with the main path passing through two gates to eventually reach a road. *Opposite is Lower Lodge – a former lodge and toll cottage which once collected fees towards local road maintenance.* Turn RIGHT.

4 Take the signposted path through a kissing gate and go up Downing Hall's former driveway. *Just beyond a kissing gate, up to your left is the remnants of the 'Fairy Oak' described by Thomas Pennant as 'a spreading oak of great antiquity, size and extent of branches'.* Continue above the stream – *near which are the remains of a line of several small fish pools.* Shortly you enter a more open aspect. *Look back at The Tower, a castellated gothic folly tower, now a private house, built in 1810.* Continue along the former driveway – *adjoining which are exam-*

ples of new species of trees, such as Monkey Puzzle tree and North American Redwood, planted in the early 19thC, by David, the son of Thomas Pennant, an avid collector of plants from around the world. Shortly you pass the remains of the once splendid Downing Hall. *Built in 1627, and the home of the Pennant family until it passed through marriage to Viscount Fielding in the 19thC, it was destroyed by fire in 1922 and demolished in 1953. The surrounding land was laid out with walks, and a series of lakes created in the nearby valley.*

5 Just beyond the ruin, at a waymarker post, turn RIGHT along a track. *Above are the stables built by Thomas Pennant in 1766.* At the wall corner, turn LEFT down below the buildings, past a path on the right to cross a stile and the stream beyond. Follow the path to a driveway. Turn LEFT and follow the driveway up through the wooded valley, soon passing a heavily silted pool on the left – *once an important estate fishery* – and on into Whitford.

MAEN ACHWYFAN

DESCRIPTION A 5 mile (**A**) or 3 mile walk (**B**) exploring the undulating countryside near Whiford and visiting two of the area's interesting ancient monuments. The main route passes through attractive estate land, then skirts woodland to reach Maen Achwyfan – a beautifully carved stone cross. It then visits a small hill within Coed y Garreg, on which stands an old stone watchtower offering panoramic views, before following field paths back to Whitford. Allow about 3 hours.
START Whitford [SJ 147782].
DIRECTIONS See **Walk 4**.

Maen Achwyfan, standing in a field just off the road, is an impressive 12 foot high circle-headed stone cross dating from about 1000 AD and named after 7thC St Cwyfan. Its carved patterns and motifs are possibly of Celtic and Viking origin. Its purpose remains subject to debate, but may be evidence of Viking settlements in the area.

From the village centre take the road signposted to Tre-Mostyn past the church, the school and Maes Rhydwen to reach a minor road on the left. (For **Walk B** simply follow this quiet country road up to the junction to visit nearby Maen Achwyfan, then rejoin the main walk from point **4**.) For **Walk A**, take a signposted bridleway ahead along a track on the right past 19thC Pennsylvania Lodge. The stony track takes you through attractive estateland. After a while, as the track bends towards another lodge, at a footpath/bridleway sign, turn LEFT off the track across pastureland to go through a gate at the end of a small plantation. Go past a hedge-lined bridleway on the right and continue along the enclosed green track past the wood – *with the watchtower on Coed y y Garreg now visible.* After a gate at the wood corner bear RIGHT along the hedge-lined track and on between farm buildings to reach a road. Turn LEFT past early 17thC Plas Uchaf.

2 At the road junction take the RIGHT fork signposted to Trelawnyd/Caerwys, then take a signposted path through an ornate iron gate on the right. Go along a green track across estateland, later bending right past a gate to go through a waymarked gate. Continue with the enclosed track and on past Pentre-ffynnon Farm to reach the bend of a road. Go along the road. Shortly, take the signposted path on the left up the access track to Pentre-ffynnon cottages. Pass in front of the cottages and cross a stile ahead. Follow the path up through the wood.

3 At a path junction, by a field corner, keep straight ahead up the narrow enclosed path running between the wood edge and the field. After a stile the path bends LEFT along the top wood edge to join an access track which you follow to the road. Turn RIGHT to the T-junction. *The small building on your right is reputed to have been a toll cottage past which coal was transported to limeworks in Denbigh.* Cross the road to visit nearby Maen Achwyfan. Return to the road and follow it RIGHT to another road junction. Take the road signposted to Whitford past the large walled boundary of Glas Coed to cross a stone stile at the end of its garden.

4 Now angle up the large field to a stile in the fence ahead, then continue in the same direction in the next field to a stile in the top corner to enter Coed y Garreg – *with good views looking back west along the coast.* At the path junction just ahead turn LEFT up to the nearby watchtower. *The inscription indicates it was a Roman pharos. In fact it is a beacon watchtower, built in the early 17thC as part of a chain that included Abergele and Deganwy to warn of pirate raids. There are extensive views along the Dee estuary, across the Wirral to Liverpool, to Cheshire, and south to the Clwydian Range.* Return to the path junction, then bear LEFT on the path opposite the stile through the wood. After crossing a stile at the wood corner, turn RIGHT along the waymarked bridleway to leave the wood at a good viewpoint. Descend between fences to the entrance to Garreg Uchaf and go down its access track. Shortly, turn sharp LEFT along another track on the

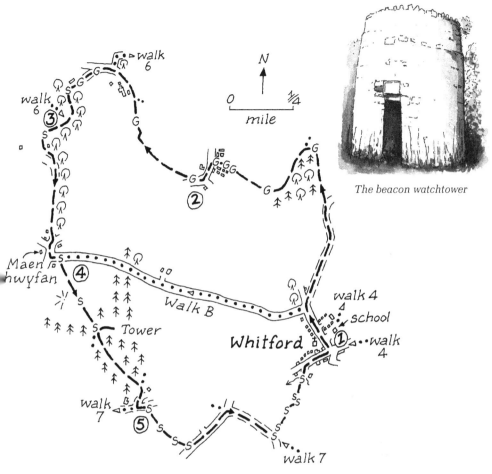

The beacon watchtower

waymarked bridleway. After 70 yards, cross a stile on the right.

5 Descend the field to a stile ahead and go along the edge of the next two fields to reach a road. Turn LEFT down the road. Later turn RIGHT on a signposted bridleway along a hedge-lined access track. Just before it bends right, cross a stile below on the left

and continue to another. Go down the field edge to a stile and across the next field to a stile ahead. Go past a wet area to a nearby hidden stile, then continue alongside the fence. At its corner, go down to a stile in the corner and another below. After a footbridge over a stream go up a driveway to the nearby road at Whitford. Follow it RIGHT back to the start.

About the author, David Berry

David is an experienced walker with a love of the countryside and an interest in local history. He is the author of a series of walks guidebooks covering North Wales, where he has lived and worked for many years, as well as a freelance writer for Walking Wales magazine. He has worked as a Rights of Way surveyor across North Wales and has served as a member of Denbighshire Local Access Forum.

GARTH & FELIN BLWM WOODS

DESCRIPTION A 4½ mile walk (**A**) featuring attractive ancient woodland. The route first passes through the narrow wooded valley of Coed-y-Garth, owned by Coed Cadw Woodland Trust, then heads towards Trelogan, with an optional diversion to a country inn. It continues past further woodland before following a quiet minor road to Tre-Mostyn. It then returns through the wooded Nant Felin Blwm. Allow about 2½ hours. Alternative 3½ mile (**B**) and 3 mile (**C**) walks are included.
START Garth Mill, near Ffynnongroyw [SJ 139817]
DIRECTIONS Entering Ffynongroyw from the east, turn off the A548 dual carriageway signposted Ffynongroyw/Pen-y-fford. Take the first turning on the left – Garth Lane – to find limited car parking just before the ford in the river to nearby Garth Mill.

*G**arth Mill** was built as a water-powered corn mill in 1743, and operated until 1956. It once ground fodder for the pit ponies that worked underground at the nearby Point of Ayr colliery. It is now an interesting country inn.*

I Cross the footbridge to pass in front of Garth Mill. Follow the track to recross the river then past a bungalow and a turning to Nant-y-Garth cottage. Keep ahead with the track, rising past further cottages, and at its end follow a path ahead into Coed y Garth. *This attractive area of woodland along the Afon y Garth is an important habitat for wildlife. It also contains a stone-lined adit driven in 1780 to drain water from the former Trelogan lead mine.* Just beyond an information board take the waymarked RIGHT fork along the top edge of the deep narrow wooded valley, later passing a reptilean sculptured bench. After being joined by a side path the main path descends to a footbridge over the river. It rises through the trees, crosses another footbridge over a side stream, then a third

footbridge over the Trelogan mine drainage adit above a small brick building. Take the stepped path up the steep wooded slope and on to a stile into a field. Turn RIGHT along the field edge, than after about 40 yards head up the field to pass to the left of tree-covered mound – *an old mine shaft of the formerTrelogan lead and zinc mine, which operated from the 18thC until the early 20thC –* to reach a stile/ gate. Continue along the green track to reach the bend of a lane by Berth-y-Maen cottage.

2 For **Walk A** follow the lane ahead to reach a T-junction at the outskirts of Trelogan. (For **Walk B/C**, turn left and follow the lane to pass through Trelogan-isaf farm. Continue along a green track to a track junction. For **Walk B** turn right towards Wern farm, then follow the driveway to the road. Turn left to rejoin the main route at point **4**. For **Walk C** keep ahead to go through a waymarked gate. Cross a nearby stile and follow the field edge past the house to a stile in the fence. Descend through trees to a footbridge amongst rhododendrons, then follow the path slightly left up the wooded slope to a stile into a field. Follow the fence on your right along the large field/wood edge to a gate, then continue along the next long field edge. As you descend the bottom corner follow the field edge round to the left above the wooded valley to a partly hidden stile in the corner. Just beyond turn right down to a large footbridge to re-enter Coed-y-Garth. Follow the path up to join your outward route.)

3 Turn RIGHT along the road. (For refreshments follow the road to the Afon Goch inn.) Otherwise, just past Stealey cottage, take a signposted path along an access track on the left to Ffrith cottage. Continue up the wide path ahead through gorse – *enjoying good views across the Dee estuary to Hilbre Island and the Wirral, and west along the coast –* to a stile/gate. Go across the field to cross stiles in the corner near a gate into Mostyn Estate land. Follow the path along the wood edge, later with trees on both sides, and passing a waymarked side path. Continue along the top edge of a steep wooded slope. At a cross-road of paths by a

field corner on your right, turn sharp LEFT to follow a path down alongside an old wall to a stile. Go past Pentre Ffynnon cottages and follow the access track to the road. Turn RIGHT, and follow this quiet country road for about ½ mile.

4 After passing the entrance to Wern farm, near houses at Tre-Mostyn, cross a stile on the left. Follow the field edge to a stile/gate in the corner. Keep ahead to another stile/gate, then follow the embanked field edge ahead to cross a stile by a gate at the top of a track. Continue along a green track, then after about 100 yards take a waymarked path by an old gate angling down into Felin Blwm wood, passing the remains of a mill. *This delightful ancient semi-natural woodland,*

has a surprising industrial past. Its Welsh name means 'lead mill', in reference to the ancient lead smelting hearths that once operated in the locality. In addition, shallow coal pits were worked in the valley during the 18th and 19th centuries. Shortly take the LEFT fork along the top edge of the wooded valley, gradually descending. After crossing a side stream/gully, the delightful path contours across the steeply wooded slopes above the river, which is soon joined by the Afon-y-Garth. The path passes above the former mill pond and cottages in the valley bottom, then the old leat which provided water for the mill. It then descends to pass behind Garth Mill, whose hospitality makes a good ending to the walk.

WALK 7

COED Y GARREG

DESCRIPTION A 6¼ mile (**A**) or 4 mile (**B**) walk following field and woodland paths through the undulating countryside around Gorsedd and Lloc, with good views The route heads to Coed y Garreg with an option to visit its 17thC hilltop watchtower. Later it passes through Coed Pen-y-Gelli to visit a Nature Reserve. Allow about 3½ hours.

START Crossroads by the Druid Inn, Gorsedd [SJ 153767].

DIRECTIONS See **Walk 3** for directions and information on Gorsedd.

I Walk west from the village centre towards Lloc. *At a rise in the road on your left are ancient burial mounds.* Continue down the road, then just before Pant y Wacco turn RIGHT along a road to reach crossroads by the Rock Inn. *Its name derives from the mining of lead and limestone in the area in the 18th/19th centuries. Note the old cast iron water pump at its rear.* Cross the road and turn RIGHT along the pavement. Go past a footpath sign at the entrance to Ty Maen, then turn LEFT on another signposted path along a track past a house. Just beyond its boundary corner turn RIGHT to follow a path through attractive woodland to eventually reach a small waymarker post. Take the path heading LEFT through the trees to leave the wood by a stile. Go across the large field to cross a stile in the far corner. Turn LEFT to go through gates and another ahead. Continue along the tree lined bridleway to reach an access track by a finger post. (For **Walk B**, turn left, signposted to Lloc, to cross a nearby stile. Go along the small field's top edge, then follow a track to Hollow Farm. Turn right to a small wooden gate, and go up a tree-lined path. Follow the path then green track to cottages. Follow the access track to the road at Lloc. Follow it right to Lloc Farm near Sion chapel. Enter the wood corner opposite to rejoin **Walk A** at point **5**.)

2 For **Walk A** continue ahead along the track – *soon with views of Coed y Garreg's hilltop watchtower, now exposed after tree-felling.* Cross the road to a bridle gate/stile. Just beyond bear RIGHT along the long field edge to go through a large gate in the corner. Follow the boundary on the left to go through a facing gate. Keep ahead to a hidden stile in the corner. Continue ahead alongside the boundary, then in the field corner by a water trough, turn LEFT up the field towards the watchtower to cross a stile in the corner. Cross the adjoining stile to enter Coed y Garreg. Now follow a bridleway LEFT along the wood edge to a waymarked bridleway/path junction at the wood corner. (To visit the watchtower cross the stile and follow the path to a crosspath at the wood edge. Bear right to the tower – see paragraph **4** of **Walk 5** for information. Return to the path junction, then either retrace your steps or continue ahead down through the wood to rejoin the main route at the lower wood edge.)

3 Keep ahead to leave the wood at a prominent viewpoint, then descend an enclosed path to the entrance to Garreg Uchaf. Go along its access track to join another. Just beyond Waen-y-Garreg cross a stone stile on the right. Go across the field, over a another stile, then follow the fence to cross a further stile, with a road nearby. Turn RIGHT past a barn to a stile into the wood. After about 100 yards, turn LEFT to follow a path along the wood edge, later joining a track to reach a road. Follow it LEFT past Gelli farm, then turn LEFT signposted to Holywell to pass Gelli Fawr – *a pre-reformation grange of Basingwerk Abbey.* About 100 yards further take a signposted path on the right. Keep ahead beside the boundary to cross a stile in it, then follow the fence to go through a gate in the corner by a stile. Go down the edge of a long field and through a gate in the corner. Go down the next field past the farm to a stile, then angle down to another stile onto the farm's access track.

4 Follow it RIGHT to the road. Go through the gate opposite and along the field edge past a pool to a stile. Keep ahead to

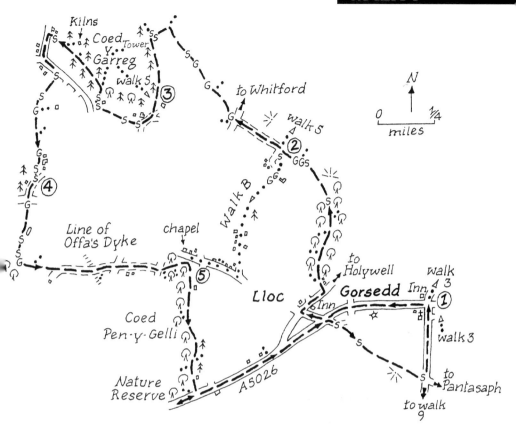

cross a stile at the wood corner. Cross the adjoining old gate and head east along a strip of enclosed rough land. Go past a stile and continue between hedges to join a farm's access track to the road – *passing over the course of Offa's Dyke.* Go along the driveway opposite and past Waen y Lloc. Continue along the track past a small duck pond. At a track T-junction turn LEFT, then go through a barrier gate on the right into a wood. Take the path angling LEFT beside the fence up to the wood corner near the road by Sion chapel. *The chapel, built in 1829, is famous for the Plygain, a unique traditional early Christmas morning service.*

5 Follow the path heading south along the edge of Coed Pen-y-Gelli, past a house, fields and later a section of conifers to join a track descending the wood edge past the cricket club pavilion to the A5026. Turn RIGHT to visit Pen y Gelli Nature Reserve – *a former limestone quarry which provided stone for local housebuilding. It contains a lime kiln used between 1790-1840 to produce lime as a fertiliser and for making lime mortar which was used to build Mostyn Docks.* Afterwards follow the road towards Lloc – *reputedly part of the Chester to Caernarvon Roman road* – then take the road into Pant y Wacco. At the side road on your outward route, take a path on the right signposted to Pantasaph. At a stile on the track's first bend keep ahead along a wide path. At an old corrugated shed, follow the path angling LEFT up the slope to a stile. Follow the boundary on your left to a road – *enjoying views of the Clwydian hills.* Follow it LEFT back into Gorsedd. *In the garden of 'The Lawns' , is one of two old standing stones unearthed when the church was built.*

WALK 8
PEN-Y-BALL
& PANTASAPH

DESCRIPTION A 4½ mile walk exploring the hills above Holywell and their industrial past, offering panoramic views. The route meanders up to Pen-y-Ball monument, erected in 1893 at a prominent viewpoint (820 feet) to commemorate the marriage of the Duke of York, heir to the throne. It then continues to Pantasaph Friary with its famous Stations of the Cross, where visitors are welcome. Shorter options are shown on the map. Allow about 3 hours
START High Street, Holywell [SJ 185759].

For centuries, the hills above Holywell were mined for lead and quarried for limestone. In the early days lead ore was smelted close to the mines in 'boles' – shallow pits dug in places exposed to strong winds, which helped fire the mixture of ore and wood. Pen-y-Ball (meaning 'bole') was once an important site for such smelting. From the mid-19thC Pantasaph became a renowned centre for Roman Catholic worship and pilgrimage, with the building of St David's church, the establishment of a Capuchin Friary, and nearby, a convent, orphanage and school. St David's was originally conceived by the Fielding family as an Anglican church, but following their conversion to Catholicism, it was opened in 1852 dedicated to the new faith. This caused much controversy, leading to unsuccessful court action by the Bishop of St Asaph, and the building of Anglican churches in nearby Brynford and Gorsedd, with public subscriptions

1 At the western end of Holywell High Street turn LEFT into Cross Street, then keep ahead up Pen y Ball Street from the Feathers Inn. At the road junction cross the road and go up Pen y Ball Hill. The road climbs steeply past houses. Just beyond the road speed signs and Westcot take a signposted path to a gate on the right into a field. (Alternatively, continue up the road to Pen-y-

Ball monument.) Continue ahead alongside the tree boundary through the bottom edge of two fields across the mine-scarred hillside – *enjoying extensive views over Holywell and the Dee Estuary* – to a stile. Follow the tree boundary on your left to go through a gap in the boundary ahead. Go across the next field to a stile in the boundary ahead. Turn LEFT up the field edge to cross a stile in the corner. Go up the middle of the field to a facing stile/gate in the top corner. Continue in the same direction up the next field to a stile by Pen-yr-Allt cottage. Turn RIGHT along the track to reach Pen-y-Ball monument – *offering views from Cheshire to Snowdonia, from Liverpool to the Clwydian Hills.*

2 Continue down the track. At a junction by Sunniside keep ahead, and after 40 yards, go half-RIGHT across tussocky ground to cross a stile. Follow the path, soon gently rising to go through a wide gap in a tree boundary. Go up the field edge to cross a stile ahead, revealing a nearby trig point. Turn LEFT and follow the stiled path along the edge of three fields – *enjoying extensive views.* Continue by a fence above a quarry, then after 10 yards bear LEFT down the field edge. *Down to your left is the remains of a 3 foot tramway opened about 1830 to carry limestone and lead ore by horse power and gravity down to Greenfield harbour. Here the line went through a tunnel in the quarry face before splitting into two branches, the main one serving the large Grange quarry. The tramway continued to provide limestone for the Holywell Lime and Cement Company's plant in the Greenfield Valley until the 1880s when the plant and Grange limestone mine closed.*

3 At the field bottom turn RIGHT to follow the old tramway towards a house. Cross a stile at its driveway and one opposite, then turn RIGHT up past the house. Just before its wall corner go half-LEFT to follow a fence through gorse and along the top of

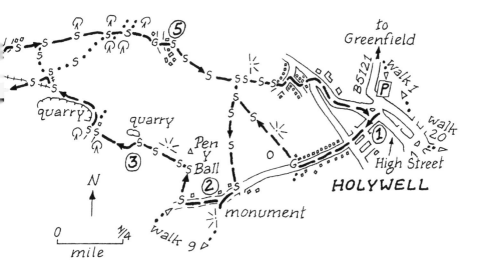

an old quarry. Later leave the fence to cross a stile in the field corner. Go half-RIGHT across the next field, then when in line with a waymarker post to your right, turn sharp LEFT and walk towards a telegraph pole to cross a stile just before it. Turn RIGHT and after a few yards angle away from the fence past gorse and across the field, then down to the field corner. Here descend through trees towards houses below. At a small gate at the rear of the houses bear RIGHT alongside the boundary to go through a small metal gate in the corner. Now go down a track to a lane by Pantasaph Friary and St. David's church. Turn LEFT, then shortly RIGHT to reach the car park and an information board.

4 Head to the village road by the former St Clare's orphanage and convent (1861-1977). Turn RIGHT. At the junction turn RIGHT. Go up the road and on the bend, cross a stile on the right. Continue beside the high wall, over another stile and on to cross a further stile at the wall corner. Turn LEFT along the field edge to a stile/gate and go past a house to rejoin the road. Take a waymarked path on the right just ahead. Go past a house to a stile and along a field to cross a stile at its end. Go along the field edge and at the boundary corner, angle LEFT down to a stone stile/ gate. Go along the

next field edge to a stile/gate, then follow a track through a wood. When it bends left keep ahead on a path to cross a stile into a field. Go along the field edge and on past a house to a gate in the corner. *Nearby is the old Grange Cavern – a 19thC limestone mine which provided stone for the construction of docks in Liverpool. Closed in 1887, it was used during the Second World War as a bomb store, including the famous dambuster 'bouncing bombs' of Barnes Wallis. For a few years after 1978 it housed an underground military museum.*

5 Cross the lane and go past the gate opposite, then take a path angling RIGHT to a hidden stile. Now follow a permissive path across the field, passing beneath a cottage and farm, to another stile. Go along the top edge of the next field to a stile in the corner. Now go half-LEFT down the field towards Holywell to cross a stile in the corner and another beyond. Go down the field, through a gateway and on down to a stile in the corner by houses to reach a road just beyond. Turn LEFT, then soon RIGHT along Bryn Aber. After 100 yards, turn LEFT down a wide pathway to a road junction. Cross the road with care and turn RIGHT past the fire/ ambulance stations and on down the road back into Holywell centre.

WALK 9

HOLYWELL COMMON & RACECOURSE

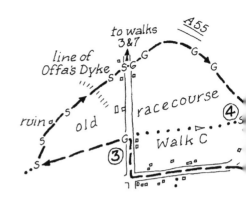

DESCRIPTION This 6¼ mile walk (**A**) explores open common, follows the route of the 18thC Holywell racecourse, visits Pen-y-Ball monument with extensive views, and offers a pleasant finish at an 19thC country inn. Allow about 3½ hours. The route includes alternative 4 mile (**B**) or 5¼ mile (**C**) walks.
START The Crooked Horn Inn, Brynford [SJ 186741].
DIRECTIONS From Holywell take the B5121 to Brynford, and at the cross-road in the village, turn left towards Pentre Halkyn to reach the Crooked Horn, where parking is allowed. Park near its inn sign.

*H*olywell Racecourse, *roughly oval in shape and over 2 miles in length, was the venue for the Holywell Hunt meetings which ran from 1767 until the mid 19thC. Horse-racing events were popular with the gentry and passionately supported by the Grosvenor family of Cheshire and the Mostyn family of North Wales.*

I Cross the road to an information board set in a large boulder. *Nearby is a National Cycle Network iron milepost.* Follow the signposted path along the stony green track onto the gorse-covered Holywell Common, soon passing a telegraph pole on your right and old workings on your left. Just beyond were old workings on your right – *with a good view ahead of Moel y Parc TV transmitter mast, and on a clear day the mountains of Snowdonia* – take a path angling back on the left. After 15 yards the path bends right, soon reaching a small rise – *with great views across the Dee estuary to Liverpool, and on a clear day north to Blackpool tower.* Continue ahead to a crossroad of five paths. Keep straight ahead towards the Clwydian Range, soon descending to a wide green cross-track. Follow it

RIGHT. Just before two cottages, bear LEFT to walk around the boundary of the left cottage, and on to join its access track. Follow it to Hafod y Bryn at the B5121.

2 Cross the road to a path opposite. Keep with the main path past a telegraph pole to reach a cross-track by the boundary corner of a cottage. Keep ahead, over a track, past a gas pipeline post, then follow path along the edge of a golf course. *In 1933, work on one of the tees revealed a Bronze Age burial site.* Cross a lane and go along the track ahead. Just before it reaches a farm entrance, bear RIGHT alongside the boundary to a lane junction at Calcoed. Continue ahead along Narrow Lane, and just before a bus shelter and a road, turn LEFT along a track. Go past Bryn Hyfryd cottage to reach a wide access track. Follow it LEFT and when it bends right, keep ahead down a green track and follow this bridleway across the common. Go over a track – (For **Walk B** follow it right to rejoin the main route at point **5**) – and continue alongside a fence. From the fence corner, keep ahead to follow the bridleway down to join a lane by the entrance to a house. Follow it to cross-roads. Turn RIGHT along the road.

3 After a few hundred yards, turn LEFT on a waymarked bridleway to begin your walk along the former Holywell racecourse. (For **Walk C** turn right just beyond, and follow another section of the racecourse to point **4**.) Follow the tree-lined bridleway for nearly ½ mile, and at a Five Villages Heritage Trail waymarker post cross

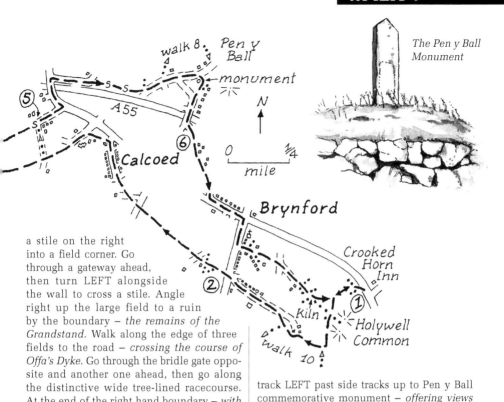

The Pen y Ball Monument

a stile on the right into a field corner. Go through a gateway ahead, then turn LEFT alongside the wall to cross a stile. Angle right up the large field to a ruin by the boundary – *the remains of the Grandstand.* Walk along the edge of three fields to the road – *crossing the course of Offa's Dyke.* Go through the bridle gate opposite and another one ahead, then go along the distinctive wide tree-lined racecourse. At the end of the right hand boundary – *with the A55 and Pantasaph ahead* – turn RIGHT to follow a green track alongside a fence to a bridle gate. Go across the slope to another bridle gate ahead, then continue with the hedged gorse strewn old racecourse.

4 Just after it bends right, cross a stile on the left, and another just ahead. Follow the field edge round for 30 yards to cross a stile. Go down the field to cross another stile and a footbridge beyond. Now follow the waymarked Heritage Trail path up the bracken slope to cross a stile. Go up the field edge to cross a stile in the corner by a farm.

5 Follow the track ahead past cottages, then turn LEFT along a road. After passing over the A55, turn RIGHT along a lane. When it bends towards a cottage follow a path ahead to a stile in a narrow boundary corner. Continue beside the boundary to another stile, then follow the path across the common. After passing a finger post follow a track LEFT past side tracks up to Pen y Ball commemorative monument – *offering views from Cheshire to Snowdonia, from Liverpool to the Clwydian Range.* From the bottom of the monument steps, bear RIGHT to descend through gorse to a track. Turn RIGHT to join a nearby lane which takes you back over the A55.

6 Immediately turn LEFT along a lane, then follow a track past houses to a road. Follow it LEFT to the crossroads in Brynford. Turn RIGHT past St. Michael's church, then at the Post Office turn LEFT along a track. As it bends half-right follow a path angling across the common. Shortly cross a track and go up a stony track ahead to pass Meifod. Continue ahead over the common, past side paths. At a path junction below a ruined lime kiln, turn LEFT, soon on your outward route back to the hospitality of the Crooked Horn. *Its name derives from the habit of an owner of this former farm who chose rams with crooked horns in lieu of rents owed by sheep farmers who leased the surrounding land.*

19

LIXWM – BRYNFORD ROUND

DESCRIPTION A 6 mile walk exploring pastureland, and open common lying between the old communities of Lixwm and Brynford. The route features impressive lime kilns and good views. Allow about 3½ hours

START Lixwm [SJ 167716].

DIRECTIONS As you enter Lixwm on the B5121 from Holywell/Brynford direction, park in a large lay-by on the bend on the right.

*L*ixwm *takes its name from Derbyshire miners who came to work in the local lead mines. They referred to their new home as a 'likesome place' and the settlement became known as 'Likesome Green'. It later became 'Licswm', then adapted its current form.*

I Follow the road through the village. Just beyond the 17thC Crown Inn's car park, take a signposted path on the left. Follow the boundary on the right round to a kissing gate into a field. Turn LEFT past another kissing gate and continue alongside the meandering tree boundary. After passing a stone ruin, cross a stile ahead, then go up the field edge. At the gate in the top corner, turn LEFT along the field edge, then pass to the left of a farm and continue ahead to a stile onto a hedge-lined lane. Follow it RIGHT, then turn LEFT along the road.

2 After passing Bryn Hyfrydd, with a telephone box ahead, turn RIGHT up a track to a stile/gate on its bend. Go up the field edge to another stile/gate, then follow the boundary on your right up the next field to go through a waymarked gap in the corner. Continue across the next field to cross a ladder-stile. Now go half-LEFT past a nearby tree/wall boundary corner. Ignore a path, and continue in the same direction across rough pasture to cross the low wall ahead and on towards the far field corner. Here cross a stile

by a telegraph pole just beyond a fenced off shaft. Now head along the long mine-capped field. Pass to the right of a pylon and continue to a stile/gate onto a road. Cross the stile almost opposite, then go half-RIGHT across the field to cross adjoining stiles, and on down to cross a stile in the corner by outbuildings. Turn LEFT along a nearby track passing in front of two 19th C stone houses. and a poultry farm.

3 When the track splits near an impressive set of five lime kilns by Pant y Pydew quarry take the LEFT fork to Waen y Brodlas. *During the 19thC, Pant y Pydew quarry provided aberdo limestone used in the building of Menai and Runcorn bridges, and docks at Liverpool and Birkenhead. Its use as a cement that set under water made it a valuable commodity. Nearby is Bryn Mawr cherstone quarry. From early last century, cherstone, used in the china-making process, was transported from here in blocks to Staffordshire.* Continue ahead with the green track past a large barn. As it bends left into a field, go half-RIGHT across an area of old workings to a good viewpoint after 70 yards. Here bear RIGHT for about 15 yards, then turn LEFT down a path through gorse. At the bottom of the slope, go half-RIGHT across an intersection of wide paths to follow the path ahead through a small area of bracken/gorse/small trees. Keep ahead , aiming for a wide green path rising up the gorse-covered slope of Holywell Common ahead, midway between two telegraph posts. Follow it up to a wide green cross-track. First continue ahead up the slope to enjoy extensive all-round views from its low summit. Now return down to the green cross-track. Follow it RIGHT and just before two cottages, bear LEFT to walk around the boundary of the left cottage.

4 About 35 yards beyond its boundary corner cross a stile on the left into a field. Go ahead down the field to pass a waymarked telegraph pole near a cottage and on down the large field towards Moel y Parc's TV transmitter mast to a stile/gate in the bottom corner. Continue to the nearby B5121. Cross the road, then bear RIGHT on a

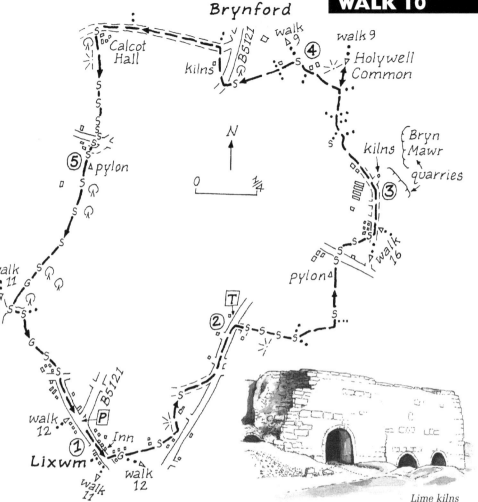

Lime kilns

signposted path, soon passing old lime kilns. At an access track, turn LEFT and follow it to Calcot Hall. Follow the track ahead past the large barn and cross a stile on the left just beyond. Go along the edge of a small wood, then the left-hand edge of a long field – *enjoying extensive views*. Cross a stile in the corner. Keep ahead, soon descending to a stile. Follow the edge of the next field round to another stile. Follow the stiled path to a road. Cross the stile opposite, then another at the rear left-hand corner the barn ahead.

5 Go up the field and on to cross a stile in its right-hand corner. Keep ahead alongside the boundary, soon descending to a stile. Continue ahead across the middle of the next four fields to eventually cross a stone stile near the final field corner to reach an enclosed bridleway near a road. Turn LEFT along the bridleway, and after about 80 yards, cross a stile on your right. Go up the field edge and through a gate in the top corner. Go up the field to clip a hedge corner and cross a stile just before a farm. Pass to the left of buildings to a stile onto a road. Go along the lane opposite past Pentre Farm, soon reaching the start.

21

YSCEIFIOG – LIXWM ROUND

DESCRIPTION A 5 mile walk (**A**) following field and woodland paths, bridleways and quiet lanes, with a choice of old country inns (check opening times in advance). The route starts from the remote ancient settlement of Ysceifiog, with its attractive 19thC church and 18thC Fox Inn, then passes through woodland near Ysceifiog lake, before heading north, providing an option to visit the 13thC Black Lion inn at Babell. The main route returns via Lixwm, with its 17thC Crown Inn. Allow about 3 hours. The route can easily be divided into two 3½ mile walks: a circuit to Babell (**B**) and a circuit to Lixwm (**C**) by using a link bridleway as shown.

START Ysceifiog [SJ 152715] or Lixwm [SJ 167716].

DIRECTIONS Ysceifiog can be reached from either the A541 or B5121. Park tidily in the village centre near the church. See **Walk 10** for the Lixwm start.

Ysceifiog, situated 600ft above sea-level, is mentioned in the Doomsday Book. It developed mainly as an agricultural community, but it has prospered from its diversity of natural resources. Limestone, lead ore, sand and gravel have been extracted here. An iron ore mine once supplied Brymbo Ironworks. Water-mills were built, wool manufacturing developed and houses were built for cotton pickers in 1792. Interestingly, Guy Fawkes stopped at Ysceifiog on his way to Holywell, shortly before the Gunpowder Plot, and witches were reported in the parish as late as 1938. In 1816, 1 mile from Ysceifiog was found one of Britain's finest bronze age gold circular torques – a collar of twisted gold 50 inches long, 14 inches wide, 20 oz in weight, of Irish origin – traditionally worn round the neck by chieftains as an insignia of power.

From the entrance to St Mary's church walk down the road to the Fox Inn. Turn RIGHT past the former school, now the Village Hall, to the junction. (For **Walk C**

keep ahead to take a signposted bridleway by the telephone box. Follow it through fields to a minor road near point **3**.) For **Walk A** turn LEFT and follow the road down into the wooded valley – *with good views of the 20 acre Ysceifiog lake created by the Earl of Denbigh in 1904 for fishing, which is still enjoyed.* Just past Drovers Tumble turn LEFT on the signposted path to Babell/Caerwys. Follow the delightful woodland path near the river and past a small pool covered by bull-rushes. At a path junction just before the lake, turn RIGHT on the path signposted to Babell/Caerwys. It rises steadily through the trees to another signposted path junction. Here bear RIGHT (Babell) and follow the undulating path through the top of the wood to eventually enter a field. Follow the boundary on your left to cross a stile by buildings and on to follow an access track to the road. Turn LEFT, then RIGHT at the junction. Bear LEFT at the next junction, then take the RIGHT fork to follow a signposted path along a track to a house.

2 Go through the waymarked gate ahead and on to cross a stile. Go along an enclosed section of path to a gate. Follow the hedge on the left through two fields to a kissing gate then go along a hedge-lined track past a farm. About 100 yards further at the tree boundary corner on your right, the path splits. (For the Black Lion inn follow the waymarked path ahead.) Otherwise turn RIGHT and descend the waymarked path initially alongside the tree boundary, then angle down across the tree-covered slope into the valley bottom. Follow the stream to a stile onto a lane. Turn RIGHT and follow the meandering lane for about ¾ mile – *later with views of the Clwydian Hills and the mountains of Snowdonia.*

3 Eventually turn LEFT on a signposted bridleway. (For **Walk B**, continue to the next bend then take the bridleway on the right. Follow it through fields to Ysceifiog.) After about 80 yards, cross a stile on your right. Go up the field edge and through a gate in the top corner. Go up the field to clip a hedge corner and cross a stile just before a farm. Pass to the left of buildings to a stile onto a road. Go along the lane opposite past Pentre Farm, soon reaching a road by modern houses just off the B5121 (the alternative start) at the outskirts of Lixwm.

low the hedge on your left, through an open gateway and along the next field to cross a stile midway. Continue with the hedge now on your right to cross a stile into a narrow hedge-lined green track. Follow it LEFT.

5 At the end of a small wood, where the track bends left, turn RIGHT on the signposted bridleway. Follow the delightful hedge then tree-lined bridleway to a road by a house. Follow it RIGHT past a nearby mainly hidden large sand/gravel quarry. Go past a bridleway leading down to Pant-y-Blodeu, then Bryn Siriol, to take a signposted path over a stile on the right. Go along

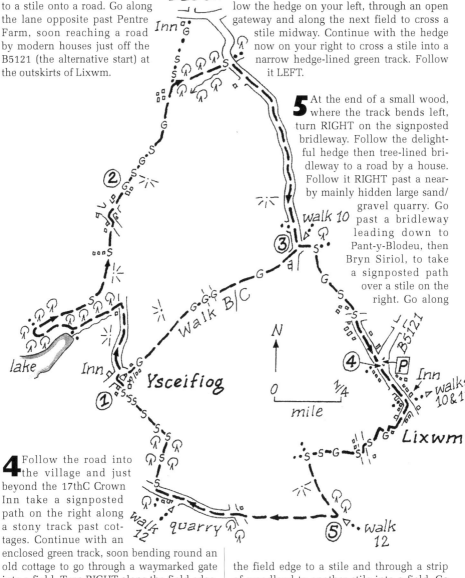

4 Follow the road into the village and just beyond the 17thC Crown Inn take a signposted path on the right along a stony track past cottages. Continue with an enclosed green track, soon bending round an old cottage to go through a waymarked gate into a field. Turn RIGHT along the field edge, through a gap in the corner, then turn LEFT along the edge of the next field. Go through an old gateway and on over a stile ahead. Follow the path down to a track by houses. Follow it LEFT for about 15 yards, then cross a stile up on the right. Bear RIGHT to fol-

the field edge to a stile and through a strip of woodland to another stile into a field. Go half-LEFT up and across the field to a stile/gate to the left of a water trough. Follow the stiled path towards Ysceifiog Church to enter the churchyard corner by a 'gravestone' stile. *Behind a tree on the right are the remains of an old preaching cross.*

WALK 12

LIXWM – NANNERCH

DESCRIPTION A 6 mile (**A**) or 4½ mile (**B**) walk exploring the attractive undulating countryside between the Wheeler Valley and Lixwm. The route descends from the attractive village of Nannerch, with its early 18thC Cross Foxes Inn, to the hamlet of Melin-y-Wern, with its old mill and Cherry Pie Restaurant. Here the route splits. Walk A meanders round both sides of the Wheeler valley before being joined by Walk B. The route then heads to Lixwm, with its 17thC Crown Inn, before following paths, tracks and quiet lanes back to Nannerch. Allow about 3½–2½ hours.
START Nannerch [SJ 166696] or Lixwm. [SJ 167716].
DIRECTIONS Nannerch lies just off the A541 Mold – St. Asaph road. Park tidily in the village centre. See **Walk 10** for the Lixwm start.

1 Go north along Village Road past the 19thC church, then turn LEFT along Ffordd y Waen. Shortly take the signposted hedge-lined byway on the right, later descending past outbuildings of a cottage and continuing to a lane at Melin-y-Wern. (For **Walk B** turn RIGHT and follow a path past cottages to reach the A541 opposite the Cherry Pie. Turn left to cross the road at a safer place then return to take a signposted path through the Cherry Pie's rear car park to cross a stile on the left. Follow the path to a stile, then along the field edge above the former water-powered mill to a stile into a wood. Follow the path up through the trees to cross two stiles at the top of the wood. Keep ahead along the field edge to a stile in the corner. At the fence corner ahead bear LEFT through a gate and on down the middle of the field to a stile in the bottom corner. Keep ahead along the field edge, then go along the green track ahead to cross a stile at a crossroad of tracks. Turn LEFT and follow the track to rejoin **Walk A**. Now follow instructions from paragraph **3**.)

2 For **Walk A** turn LEFT along the lane to a T-junction. (To shorten the walk follow the road right past Sarn Mill Fisheries.) Take the signposted path ahead along the wood edge near the river to eventually reach a field. Continue along its bottom edge, then just after a telegraph pole (120 yards), turn RIGHT up to a stile onto a narrow road. Turn RIGHT up the road, then take a signposted path through a gate on the right opposite Fron House. Follow the hedge-lined path to cross a stile by Pen-yr-erw. Keep ahead then at the cottage's boundary corner go half-LEFT across a field to go through an old gateway in the tree boundary. Follow the level path across the steep-sloped field. After about 120 yards, angle RIGHT down through a large gap between holly trees and continue down the slope – *with a view of Sarn in the valley* – to cross a stile in the fence below. Follow a path LEFT down to a small gate and on down the field edge to a gate, then to a stile onto a road. Follow it down to cross over the former Mold – Denbigh railway line and river Wheeler at Sarn to reach the A541. Go up the road opposite, signposted to Ysceifiog, then take a signposted bridleway up a track on the right past houses to reach a lane. Follow it RIGHT and just beyond a house take a signposted bridleway on the left. Follow this delightful tree-lined bridleway to meet a track (**Walk B**) by a small wood. Here turn LEFT.

3 Continue along the narrow hedge-lined green track to a road by a farm. Turn LEFT and immediately RIGHT along a signposted bridleway past a house and a cottage. Continue along the bridleway (can be muddy). Later, just beyond a second stile on the left, cross a stile on the right. Go along the field edge to cross a stile in the corner, then go through a gate in the corner ahead. Go along the field edge to a stile in the corner, then along the next field edge. In the corner at a path junction by houses turn LEFT to follow the field wall to cross a stone stile to reach a road (the alternative start) just off the B5121 at the outskirts of Lixwm.

4 Follow the road into the village to the 17thC Crown Inn – *a good refreshment*

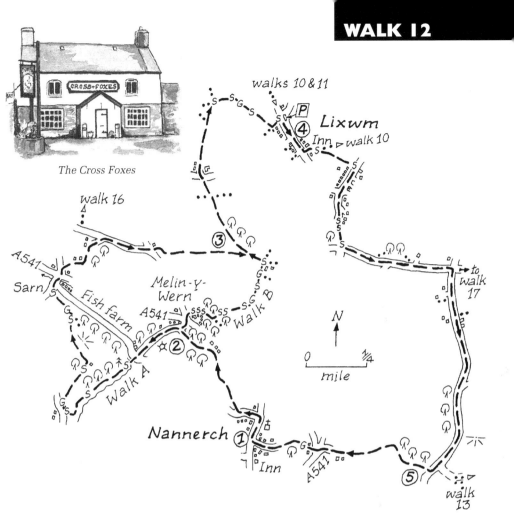

The Cross Foxes

stop. Just beyond its car park, take a sign-posted path on the left. Follow it round to a kissing gate into a field. Go half-LEFT to pass a tree boundary corner and continue across the large undulating field past gorse to a stile in the far field corner by a house. Follow the road RIGHT past houses and when it bends right keep ahead along an access lane. Follow it past turnings to houses to cross a stile at its end into a field. Cross a stone stile ahead and follow the path near the boundary on your left to a stile onto a road. Follow it LEFT for ½ mile to a junction. Here turn RIGHT and follow the narrow attractive hedge-lined country road past houses. Later the road rises to the entrance to Ffagnallt, then continues

past a wood. Shortly you pass a track on the left (a link with **Walk 13**).

6 About 150 yards further, turn RIGHT down a hedge-lined green track past a wood. Continue with the track to Pant-y-Ffuan, then follow its access lane to the A541. Cross the road with care to take a signposted path over a footbridge opposite and through a small gate by a cottage. Follow the path up to another small gate and up through trees then between hedges to reach a lane at Nannerch. Follow it past a school and houses to reach Village Road and nearby Cross Foxes Inn.

25

COED-Y-FELIN & MOEL Y GAER

DESCRIPTION A 6¼ mile walk (**A**) exploring the varied countryside lying between the Wheeler valley and Halkyn Mountain, featuring the attractive ancient woodland of Coed-y-Felin and Coed Trellyniau, both managed by North Wales Wildlife Trust, the small 18thC settlement of Moel-y-crio, and Moel y Gaer Iron-Age hillfort. Allow about 3½ hours. Also included are an alternative 4¼ mile walk (**B**) and a 1¼ mile circuit of Coed-y-Felin (**C**)

START Coed-y-Felin, Hendre [SJ196678].

DIRECTIONS As you enter Hendre from Mold on the A541, take a discreet side road on the right just before the first houses to find the informal parking area after about 150 yards.

1 Enter Coed y Felin by a stile/gate and follow the path ahead soon passing through a small gate. Go up the stepped path, then descend through the trees to a path junction. Take the wide path angling up through the wood, later levelling out. At a path junction keep ahead through a fence gap, and on into a side valley to join a wider path coming in from the left. (For **Walk C** or for refreshments at the nearby Royal Oak inn, turn sharp left down this path. Soon, turn left past an information board along the former Mold-Denbigh railway line (1886-1963). At a crossroad of paths, keep ahead on a narrowing path to cross a stile. Turn left and follow the path back up to the start.)

2 For **Walks A/B** follow the new path up to the wood end, then go along a hedge-lined track past Cilcain Hall – *the seat of a branch of the prominent Mostyn family until 1873* – to eventually reach a road. Go along the road, past the entrance to Fron Farm caravan park, then take a signposted hedge-lined path on the left to a stile into a field. Follow the hedge on your right round to a stile in the corner. Now go half-LEFT across the next field to a stile into the corner of Coed Trellyniau. Continue ahead near the wood's right-hand boundary to cross a stile in its far corner. Turn LEFT and follow the tree boundary on your right, soon descending. Now turn LEFT to cross a stile in the boundary on your right onto a hedge-lined track. Follow it RIGHT for about ½ mile.

3 At a lane, turn LEFT. (For **Walk B**, turn right to rejoin the main walk at point **6**.) Follow it past Rhewl then a farm complex. At a large barn where the lane descends to a house, go half-RIGHT up a green track. After 15 yards bend sharp RIGHT up to cross a stile by a finger post. Go up the field edge, over a 'gate' in the corner, then follow the boundary on your left to cross a stile in the corner. Turn RIGHT along the field edge for about 100 yards, then go half-LEFT to a stile/gate onto a road. Follow it up to a road junction, then go along the road signposted to Rhosesmor up through Moel-y-Crio to pass the village well by a bus shelter. *Halkyn Mountain has few springs and natural ponds. Expanding communities were served by wells, often connected by a network of paths. In the 1930s, standpipes were widely established and many wells collapsed or were filled in. Their importance is illustrated by the fact that in 1912, youths from Warrington were fined 16 shillings for vandalising this particular one.* Continue along the road.

4 At a track just beyond Hillside Cottage, angle LEFT across open ground and an access track. Go across the common passing to the left of a fenced shaft and on near a track leading to a large stone house with Scots pines. Continue near its boundary fence. At its corner keep ahead to follow a green track past a telegraph pole. At a track junction follow a path ahead to reach a tree/hedge corner. Keep ahead to reach a lane near River View. Follow it RIGHT past cottages. At a lane/track crossroads, keep ahead along a track past Hawthorn cottage to enter the common. To avoid bank erosion ahead, bear LEFT then after about 15 yards turn RIGHT up the slope to pass a double tele-

Walk 12

Coed Trellyniau

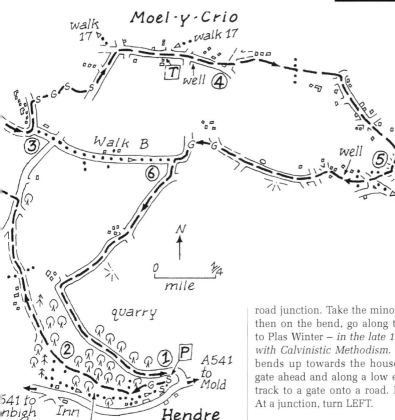

Moel-y-Crio

graph pole. Soon take its right fork up to the western ramparts of Moel y Gaer – *offering extensive views across the Dee estuary to Liverpool.* (See **Walk 15** for details of the fort). Follow the ramparts south – *with new views of the Clwydian Range.*

5 Just before the reservoir mound on your left, turn RIGHT (west) down to a nearby telegraph pole. Here angle LEFT down a path through gorse to two small metal posts by a stony track. Now go half-RIGHT across the track to follow a path down through gorse to reach a holly hedge/fence corner. Keep ahead with the hedge/tree boundary on your right to pass an old well, then water pump. Pass between a cottage and an outbuilding and go along its access track. Where it meets another, turn LEFT to walk down open ground to a

road junction. Take the minor road opposite, then on the bend, go along the access drive to Plas Winter – *in the late 18thC associated with Calvinistic Methodism.* When the track bends up towards the house, go through a gate ahead and along a low embanked green track to a gate onto a road. Follow it LEFT. At a junction, turn LEFT.

6 Follow this quiet country road to a T-junction by 18thC Hendre farm – *occupied in 1882 by the manager of Hendre lead mines.* Turn RIGHT and follow the road by the landscaped perimeter of Hendre quarry, soon on a steady descent towards the Wheeler valley and the start. *Hendre quarry has produced stone and lime for agricultural and industrial purposes, since the 1870s. It was transported from a siding on the adjoining Denbigh-Mold railway to markets in NW England. Between 1939-69, high grade limestone was mined from underground chambers, via Olwyn Goch lead-mining shaft just to the east, mainly to supply Pilkingtons of St Helens for use in glassmaking. The 470 foot deep shaft facilitated the extraction of lead and zinc from the mid-point of the Milwr tunnel from the 1930s until 1977. During World War II, TNT was stored in side tunnels.*

WALK 14

AROUND GWYSANEY

DESCRIPTION A 6 mile walk (**A**) through the undulating countryside between Rhosesmor and the outskirts of Sychdyn, exploring the lush wooded Gwysaney Estate, with its early 17thC Hall. There is an opportunity to enjoy the hospitality of the Red Lion, a small traditional country inn (telephone 01352 780570 for opening times). Allow about 3½ hours. An alternative 3¾ mile walk (**B**) is included..

START Red Lion, Rhosesmor [SJ 213681].

DIRECTIONS The Red Lion is at the southern end of Rhosesmor on the B5123. Parking is allowed by kind permission of the owner, but park at the rear of the car park to avoid blocking access for a truck.

*R*hosesmor, *lying at the eastern end of Halkyn Mountain on the 17thC Shrewsbury-Holywell road, expanded greatly during the 19thC lead-mining boom. Mines and lead-processing works once dominated the site of the current industrial estate.*

I From the entrance to the Red Lion follow the signposted path along the track leading away from the road. Follow it past a garage workshop and a house to cross a stiled gate ahead into a field. Follow the boundary on the left – *with extensive views over the Dee to Merseyside, to the distant Beeston Castle in Cheshire, and Hope Mountain to the south west* – to cross a stile near the corner. Go through a waymarked gate ahead (Wat's Dyke Way) then turn RIGHT along the field edge to a gate in the corner. Go along a farm track, through another gate, then just before the farm, take a signposted path over a stone stile on the right to join a nearby road. Continue along the road past side roads then descending past the large farm of Gwern y Mar. Go down the road's left fork, soon bending left.

2 Shortly, take a signposted path through the second gate on the right. Go across the field, passing to the right of a large single tree and on past the corner of the wood ahead. Follow the field edge up to a stile in the corner. Go along the edge of the next field to a stile in the bottom corner. Turn RIGHT to follow the waymarked bridleway along a hedge-lined track, later entering an area of mature mixed woodland. When it does a U – turn right keep ahead to join a waymarked Flintshire Circular walk. (For **Walk B** follow the track up to Quarry Farm, then cross two stiles to enter a field to rejoin the main walk at point **5**.) Follow the path through the trees, soon descending LEFT to cross a sleeper bridge. Go through a small area of conifers, over another small footbridge, and on through mixed woodland to reach a track.

3 Follow it RIGHT through Big Wood to reach a stile/ gate. Continue along the track – *enjoying more open aspects across the part wooded valley, with Gwysaney Hall prominent on the skyline This fine Welsh country House, built by Robert Davies in the early 17thC, has had a chequered history. It was attacked by Roundheads during the Civil War, then abandoned for 200 years, before being restored. Soon you will glimpse a lake in the valley bottom. Eventually the track reaches a road by an estate cottage. Turn RIGHT along the road.*

4 At a junction, take a signposted path through a gate on the right by Blackbrook Cottage. Now follow the hedge-lined green track, rising steadily, to eventually go through a gate by Tan-y-Wal. Continue up the track alongside a wood, later bending left – *giving a good view of Gwysaney Hall.* Go across its driveway and down a green track to go through a gate ahead near a cattle grid to join an access track beyond. Follow it RIGHT. After crossing a stile by a cattle grid near a house, cross another stile in the wooden fence ahead, then follow the path round the left hand edge of a small tree-lined pool to rejoin the track. Turn RIGHT, and after a few yards turn LEFT along a green track near the high red bricked perimeter wall. After a kissing gate continue along the green track beside the stone wall. Go through another kissing gate and on through Ram Wood, soon descending to a stile/gate at the wood edge

Go along the next field edge to a stile onto a road. Cross the stile opposite and go along the field edge. After a squeeze stile/gate in the field corner, turn LEFT up the next field

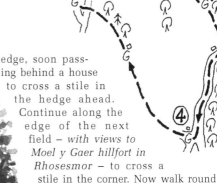

Rhosesmor

into a field. Continue ahead beside the fence – *with good open views towards Cheshire and Merseyside* – soon descending to the field corner above a house to be joined by **Walk B**. Turn LEFT.

5 Go up the field edge and on to cross a stile/footbridge ahead by a telegraph pole. Continue ahead across the reedy field towards the hilltop house to a broken stile/gap in the boundary ahead. Bear half-RIGHT across the field passing beneath the house to cross a stile in the fence. Go ahead across the middle of a steeply banked field and up the slope ahead to cross a stile onto the house's access track. Go up the track, then cross a stile on the bend. Go ahead across the field, and just beyond a solitary tree to your left after about 100 yards, turn RIGHT to pass a hedge corner to cross a stile ahead.

edge, soon passing behind a house to cross a stile in the hedge ahead. Continue along the edge of the next field – *with views to Moel y Gaer hillfort in Rhosesmor* – to cross a stile in the corner. Now walk round the edge of the next very large field – *enjoying views across to the Clwydian Range* – to join your outward route in the field corner by a house. Follow it back for refreshments at the Red Lion.

Gwysaney Hall

29

CWM CONWY & MOEL Y GAER

DESCRIPTION A 6 mile walk (**A**) through undulating countryside and the wooded Conwy valley, finishing on Moel y Gaer Iron-Age hillfort, offering extensive views. The route incorporates sections of the medieval trading route from Chester to Denbigh, used by travellers and pack ponies, later becoming part of the London-Holyhead Post road, and a section of the old Chester–Holywell coaching road. Allow about 3½ hours. Alternative 2½ mile (**B**), 4½ mile (**C**), and 3¾ mile (**D**) walks are described.

START Rhosesmor [SJ 214684].

DIRECTIONS In Rhosesmor turn off the B5123 on the road signposted to Northop, to park near a childrens' play area.

B *eneath Rhosesmor is a large cavern about 150 feet high, containing two lakes of clear blue water, over 200 feet deep. It was discovered in 1932 by Capt. Jack Francis, a mining engineer, who had to rescue two men, whose makeshift raft collapsed whilst surveying the lakes. In 1937, a raft made of empty oil barrels being used by geologists inspecting the lakes, similarly capsized. Fortunately only their pride was hurt.*

Above the village, at a height of 994 feet, stands Moel y Gaer hillfort, 600 feet in diameter, with entrance, guard chambers, ramparts and ditches. Excavations undertaken in 1972–74 during the construction of a reservoir within the fort, revealed evidence of earlier Neolithic and Bronze Age occupation. Also found was the site of a fire beacon built in 1814 to warn of any French threat from the sea during the war with Napoleon. It is said that in 1403, Hywel Gwynedd set up a camp on the hill during his support of Owain Glyndŵr's revolt.

1 Continue along the road, and after about ⅓ mile, on a bend, take a signposted path to cross a stile ahead. Keep ahead to cross another stile, then follow the hedge on your left – *with good views across the*

Dee estuary – to cross a wooden fence in the field corner. Descend to a gate by a stream, then go up a farm track and through another gateway. Go across the next field to a stile/gate. Now angle LEFT down to an old tree in a boundary corner. Keep with the boundary on your left to cross a hidden stile in it. Turn RIGHT along the field edge to a stile onto a lane. Follow it LEFT to a junction by a house. (For **Walks B** and **C** turn left – *the ancient route* – to the next junction by a farm. For **Walk B** follow the lane ahead to point **4**. For **Walk C**, cross a stile on the right. Follow a path across three undulating fields to reach a track by the end of a wood. Follow it left to point **3**.)

2 For **Walk A**, turn RIGHT, then after a few yards RIGHT again down a track. *This is the Post road.* Follow it down to a house and continue ahead on the old route, now a path, soon rising then descending to a road. (For **Walk D** follow the road left up past Bryn Eithin farm entrance. Just beyond the next house, take the track ahead to point **3**.) Turn RIGHT to reach a road junction by Middle Mill. Take the signposted path through the gate opposite and descend half-RIGHT – *note the ruin, one of three former mills on the river Conwy* – to follow the line of the old road down to a confluence of streams. *The old road crossed the stream by a pack horse bridge or ford and continued to Northop.* Just beyond bear LEFT to cross a stile and a nearby footbridge over the Afon Conwy. Turn LEFT and follow a stiled path near the Conwy along the attractive wooded valley. Eventually you reach a wooden fence below the busy A55. Follow it LEFT down to cross a stile above the stream, then climb steeply up the field to cross a waymarked section of wooden fence. Turn LEFT up the long field edge to a stile in the corner and on to the road above. Turn RIGHT along the pavement on the former A55 – *enjoying good views across the Dee estuary.* Shortly, go up a signposted hedge-lined bridleway on the left . At a cross-track turn RIGHT.

3 Follow the track along the wood edge and on to reach a lane by a house. Follow it ahead. *The track and lane are part*

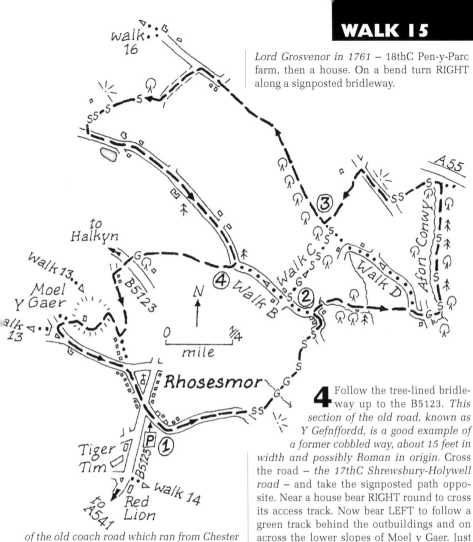

Lord Grosvenor in 1761 – 18thC Pen-y-Parc farm, then a house. On a bend turn RIGHT along a signposted bridleway.

4 Follow the tree-lined bridleway up to the B5123. *This section of the old road, known as Y Gefnffordd, is a good example of a former cobbled way, about 15 feet in width and possibly Roman in origin.* Cross the road – *the 17thC Shrewsbury-Holywell road* – and take the signposted path opposite. Near a house bear RIGHT round to cross its access track. Now bear LEFT to follow a green track behind the outbuildings and on across the lower slopes of Moel y Gaer. Just before you reach a track by Rock Cottage, do a sharp U-turn to follow a path up past the edge of a quarry to its top. Continue up through gorse onto the upper ramparts of the hillfort, offering extensive views. Turn LEFT – *with views towards the Clwydian Range* – and follow the ramparts round the southern side of the fort. After passing the reservoir mound, descend LEFT down a green slope to a telegraph pole, then angle LEFT down between gorse to a track. Follow it LEFT, then continue along the road past Foel farm and a lime kiln, later bearing RIGHT to reach the B5123. Go along the road opposite to the start.

of the old coach road which ran from Chester via Halkyn to Holywell, until its replacement by the original A55 built in 1826-7. Shortly turn LEFT on a signposted path up Midlist farm's driveway, passing through what was a large park until the early 18thC. As it begins to bend left, turn RIGHT to follow a waymarked path up the edge of a small wood to cross a stile. Follow telegraph poles up the field to a stile – *with good views looking back.* Keep ahead along the field edge to a stile, then descend to another below. Just beyond bear LEFT alongside the tree/hedge boundary to a road. Follow it LEFT for ¾ mile passing a small lake, a high stone wall – *the boundary of a deer park created by*

31

WALK 16

HALKYN, LIMESTONE & LEAD

DESCRIPTION A fascinating 6 mile (**A**) or 3¾ mile (**B**) walk that provides a great insight into the history of Halkyn and the industrial development of Halkyn Mountain. Allow about 3½ hours.

START Upper Halkyn [SJ 208706].

DIRECTIONS Follow the B5123 through Rhosesmor to Halkyn. After passing the Bluebell Inn, take the first turning left to park tidily in the village centre.

*H*alkyn *is an ancient settlement mentioned in the Domesday Book. Upper Halkyn, previously known as Catch, developed during the 18thC and 19thC lead-mining booms. In 1704 the Grosvenors purchased Halkyn Hall estate and by the 19thC had become the largest local landowner. With a passion for horse-racing, in the mid 18thC, they built large stables and created a race track on the mountain. In 1824-27, Halkyn Castle was built as their new country house, where friends were entertained after visits to Holywell racecourse. It was sold in 1913. The castle development led to the demolition of part of the original village. A new church and school were built nearby, financed by the Grosvenors.*

I Just before the Post Office bear LEFT down a stony track to the B5123. Turn RIGHT then take a signposted path on the left. Go along the field edge to enter Castle Wood. Take the main path down through the attractive woodland to a stile into a field at a good viewpoint. Go down the field to a stile by Caeau Gleision, then turn LEFT past the house to another stile. Just beyond join a green track, which rises gently to join another. After about 30 yards, turn RIGHT to follow a path through open woodland to a stile into a field. Head across to a stile, then go along the wood edge past Ty Llwyd to the road by the old churchyard. *The house opposite was once the village police station. Nearby is the Brittania Inn, the last of four*

local inns, which once housed an abattoir.

2 Go up the road to the junction by the Church built in 1878. *Opposite is the old school, built in 1849 and enlarged in 1898/9, which once had about 200 pupils.* Turn LEFT to go through a nearby kissing gate. Go along the edge of three fields and on to reach the driveway to nearby Old Hall. Continue ahead along an access track to its end at the entrance to Halkyn Old Hall – *the site of the original Grosvenor mansion demolished in the early 19thC. Old Hall and Halkyn Old Hall were formerly stables with accommodation for jockeys and grooms, later converted into houses for the new mines cashier and mine agent who came from Cornwall. The castellated folly higher up was the estate workshop.* Go through a small gate and across the driveway to Halkyn Old Hall Mews and over the stile opposite. Go along an enclosed path, then the edge of a small wood, soon bearing LEFT to reach the entrance to a large embanked compound.

3 Turn RIGHT, then after a few yards LEFT up the edge of another wood to a stile/gate. Go up the slope and on up the field towards a transmitter mast, later bending RIGHT to a stile, then to another onto Fron Farm's gated driveway. After negotiating the locked gate by stile and gate keep ahead toward the mast across the common to a telephone box in the hamlet of Windmill – *named after a windmill that once stood to the east.* Turn RIGHT along the former 17thC Shrewsbury-Holywell road. Just past the road speed sign, bear LEFT up a track. After passing around the wall corner by outbuildings of Roseberry Villa, angle away from the track along a wide path rising gently through gorse to reach a crossroad of paths at a panoramic viewpoint. (For **Walk B** continue ahead down across the common to reach the road by Rhes-y-cae school.)

4 Turn RIGHT along the broad ridge to reach a trig point – *offering extensive views.* Continue along the ridge, later descending past a pylon to a road. Turn RIGHT, then at the junction LEFT down the road towards Lixwm. *From the early 19thC the nearby quarry produced limestone for*

kilns and buildings, and cherstone, used in the china-making process in the Potteries. *It now*

towards Halkyn out of the village. *On the left were open-cast workings and a leat which conveyed water used in the lead separation process.*

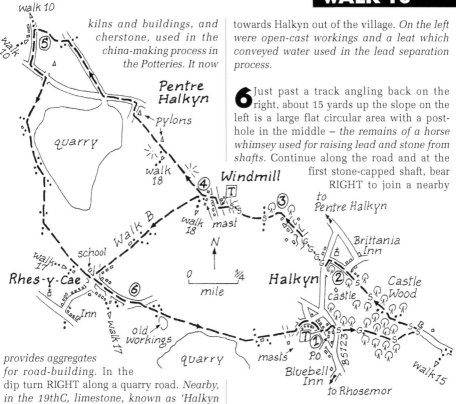

6 Just past a track angling back on the right, about 15 yards up the slope on the left is a large flat circular area with a post-hole in the middle – *the remains of a horse whimsey used for raising lead and stone from shafts.* Continue along the road and at the first stone-capped shaft, bear RIGHT to join a nearby parallel path. Soon take the RIGHT fork, over a cross-track and on up to pass fenced-off old workings. *Here fire clay was extracted in the late 19thC for use in the Staffordshire Potteries. Ahead lies Pant quarry, which in the 19thC produced stone used for buildings, gateposts, grave headstones, and for lime. It greatly expanded in the 1960s. Stone-capped mine shafts adorn the landscape.* Continue towards two transmitter masts ahead – *past the remains of a pool which supplied water used to separate ore from stone* – and on past the quarry perimeter fence. *To your left was Pen-y Bryn deep shaft into the Milwr tunnel, whose distinctive head-frame was removed in 1987.* Just before the fence corner, go up half-LEFT, over a cross-track and along a track passing just to the left of cottages. At the boundary corner keep ahead up the common, passing several cross-paths, later descending a track by a wall, then a lane to the road in Upper Halkyn.

provides aggregates for road-building. In the dip turn RIGHT along a quarry road. *Nearby, in the 19thC, limestone, known as 'Halkyn marble' because it could be polished, was quarried. It was used for fireplaces and as pillars in the new Halkyn church.* The road passes under electricity cables, then rises and levels out. *To your right is Pen-yr-henb-las cherstone quarry dating from 1838.* After a cross-path take a wide path angling LEFT past capped mine shafts to reach houses.

5 Follow the access lane LEFT to the road. Turn LEFT, then shortly RIGHT along a track At a house keep alongside the fence of the landscaped quarry, then at the fence corner take the wide RIGHT fork passing beneath an embankment. After about 150 yards, take a green track angling RIGHT across the common and over a cross-track. At the top of a small rise, take the LEFT fork towards Rhes-y-cae, later joining a stony track to reach a road junction by the school. *Sited nearby until the late 19thC were several large steam engine houses used to pump up water from the mines.* Follow the road ahead

WALK 17

MOEL FFAGNALLT

DESCRIPTION A 3¼ mile walk exploring the area between Rhes-y-cae, which stands on the 18thC Chester–Denbigh coach road, and Moel-y-Crio, featuring the small hill of Moel Ffagnallt (942 feet), offering panoramic views. The walk can easily be started from Rhes-y-cae itself by joining the route from the road junction by the primary school. Allow about 2 hours.
START Just west of Rhes-y-cae [SJ 184711].
DIRECTIONS From Rhes-y-cae follow the road towards Lixwm past Christ church. Just beyond a cattle-grid sign is an off-road parking area on the right.

I Go along the road towards Rhes-y-cae, then take a signposted path angling away on the left, soon becoming a green track and rising across the common. At a field boundary corner keep with the left fork, past side paths, to join a stony track by a white cottage ahead. Turn LEFT and follow the track to reach a road junction by Rhes-y-cae primary school. Continue along the road ahead towards Halkyn. After about 200 yards take a rough lane on your right to pass between cottages, then follow a path angling off the track towards Moel Ffagnallt. As you near the road, turn LEFT up a part stony track. About 50 yards beyond a fenced-off shaft turn RIGHT along a path then LEFT through bracken and gorse to cross a stile. Go up the field to another stile, and continue up the next long field, soon by the perimeter fence of the quarry. Go past a stile to another in the fence corner. Continue up to a stile in the next corner.

2 Keep ahead, then bear LEFT up a path to pass behind outbuildings, then follow a stony track round past other outbuildings. *At the bend a stile to the left gives access to a dramatic view into the vast layered quarry. Heed the warning signs!* Follow the track past houses, then as it bends left, go ahead across the common to a telephone box by

the road at Moel-y-Crio. Continue along the road. On the bend take the road signposted to Cilcain, then turn RIGHT up a stony track. After about 120 yards, take a path on the right between boulders. Follow it up the eastern slope of Moel Ffagnallt to reach its summit. *Here are superb all-round views. Just below on its northern slopes is a stone cairn/viewing platform – part of an award-winning environmental scheme organised by Rhes-y-cae and Moel-y-Crio communities to mark the millennium – under which is buried a time capsule.*

3 Now head west from the summit to follow a path along its rocky edges. Soon bend RIGHT down a path past gorse. *One mile to the west is Ffagnallt Hall. According to legend, in the 19thC, a maid threw a skull reputed to be of Dafydd, one of the last Welsh Princes into its pond. After a night of weird disturbances, she returned it to the house, where it still remains.* At the bottom of the slope bear RIGHT down a green track through gorse, soon joining a stony track which descends the hillside. When it bends right to the road, continue ahead across the common to join the road at the outskirts of Rhes-y-cae. Soon, bear LEFT past a farm along a minor road. Follow it past another farm, then at a signposted cross-path cross a stile on the right. Follow the hedge round to another stile, and continue along the next field edge, gradually descending to a stile onto the road by the start.

WALK 18

A BREATH OF FRESH AIR

DESCRIPTION An exhilarating 2 mile walk across central Halkyn Mountain once extensively worked for limestone, firestone and especially lead in open-cast workings and deep mines served by several engine houses. A high viewpoint and great sense of space. The wild open grassy landscape is the result of centuries of continuous grazing by cattle and sheep under commoners rights held by property owners.

Allow about 1½ hours. The walk can easily be started from Rhes-y-cae itself by joining the route just beyond the village school.
START East of Rhes-y-cae [SJ 199710].
DIRECTIONS From the road junction by Rhes-y-cae school, take the road signposted to Halkyn. Shortly after passing limekilns on your left is a small off-road parking area by a finger post.

1 Follow the road back towards Rhes-y-cae, soon passing an old quarry. Just beyond the old limekilns, turn RIGHT to follow a path running between stone-capped shafts. Keep ahead on the main path to pass two large concrete posts. The path now heads north-west then continues along the right-hand edge of a cutting/old workings, becoming a more distinct green track. When it reaches the road near a children's play area and Rhes-y-cae Primary School turn RIGHT.

2 After about 200 yards, at an informal car parking area, turn RIGHT along a green track, parallel with your outward route. At a crossroad of paths after about 150 yards, turn LEFT and follow a path through old workings. Keep ahead on the left fork and follow the path up to the trig point soon vis-

ible on the horizon ahead. *Here are extensive all-round views from the Clwydian Hills to Liverpool, Cheshire to Snowdonia.* Now head south-east along the broad ridge towards a distant single transmitter mast at Windmill. When in line with the mast to your left take the wide right fork of the path heading towards a distant quarry. At a cross-path keep ahead, passing a cottage 100 yards to your left, and heading towards twin transmitter masts. At a telegraph pole (071510910) – *with a view of Halkyn ahead* – turn RIGHT down a green track to the start.

35

WALK 19

GADLYS & NANT-Y-FLINT

DESCRIPTION A 7 mile walk (**A**) exploring the undulating attractive rural hinterland between Bagillt and Flint, featuring the wooded Nant-y-Flint valley, and good views. Allow about 4 hours. An alternative described 3 mile walk (**B**) is included.
START Bagillt [SJ 219753].
DIRECTIONS Turn off the A548 Flint – Rhyl dual carriageway into Bagillt to reach a public car park adjoining The Stag Inn. There is alternative car parking opposite the library.

*B*agillt *developed during the 18th and 19th centuries as an important industrial centre, boasting collieries, lead and chemical works, and a brewery, due to the local availability of coal, lead and river then rail transport facilities.*

I Go up nearby Gadlys lane, passing to the left of the library, then take the first road on the left. Follow the narrow road past houses to a T-junction. Turn RIGHT and at the junction with Old London Road cross a stile ahead. Just beyond take the path's right fork to cross a stream and continue up the rough field to a stile in the corner by a large barn. Cross the stile opposite, and go up the field to a stile between trees. Continue along the left hand slope of a shallow valley up to a stile in the corner. Keep ahead beside the hedge to a stile in the top corner. *It is hard to imagine this tranquil rural location of Gadlys was the site of a prestigious lead smelting and silver refining works in the 18thC. Lead from here was sent by ship to Plymouth and London. Just to the south lies early 17thC Gadlys Hall, and nearby is the site of a famous battle in 1157, when Henry II had to retreat from Welsh forces. The area is known as Bryn Dychwelwch (Hill of Return).* Turn RIGHT along the access track to rejoin Gadlys lane.

2 Turn LEFT and follow the attractive lane up the hillside, later passing Bryn Madyn Hall (1730). At a T-junction, turn LEFT and shortly cross a stile on the right, waymarked Wat's Dyke Way. Go ahead across the field and down to a stile into a wood. Descend through trees then just above a house the path bends LEFT down to a stile. Follow the access track to a road. (For **Walk B** follow the road left and just past Fferm farm before a bend, take a signposted path through a gate on the right. Follow the boundary round to a stile. Continue along the field edge to another stile. Follow the field edge round to pass along the top of a densely wooded valley to cross a stile in the corner. *Further up the wood is the site of Hen Blas castle, where Welsh princes once resided, and where the Celtic King Cenwalf of Mercia died in 810 AD.* Go down the field edge and at a footbridge turn left and continue from point 5).

3 For **Walk A** go along Nant Road opposite. Follow it through a delightful rural backwater, past a 19thC chapel, cottages and Nant Farm. *The road runs below the line of Wat's Dyke, built around 700 AD by the Mercian King Aethelbad, as a frontier boundary.* At the T-junction turn RIGHT and cross a stile on the left. Follow the path by the fast flowing Nant-y-Flint to another stile, then along the top edge of the attractive narrow wooded valley, past a waymarked path junction. Later the waymarked path crosses a more open area – *with Plas-isaf on the skyline* – then passes through gorse to a stile into a wood. The path rises through the trees, then continues below the top wood edge. At a waymarked path junction, take the right fork across the wooded slope. After a while the path passes through a dense area of rhododendron, then descends to cross stiles and a large footbridge over the river. Continue along the right bank of the river, later on a green track, to reach the bend of a stony track by a black and white building. Here do a sharp U-turn LEFT to follow a signposted path down to cross another large footbridge over the river and up through the trees. At a path junction keep ahead up to a stile into a field.

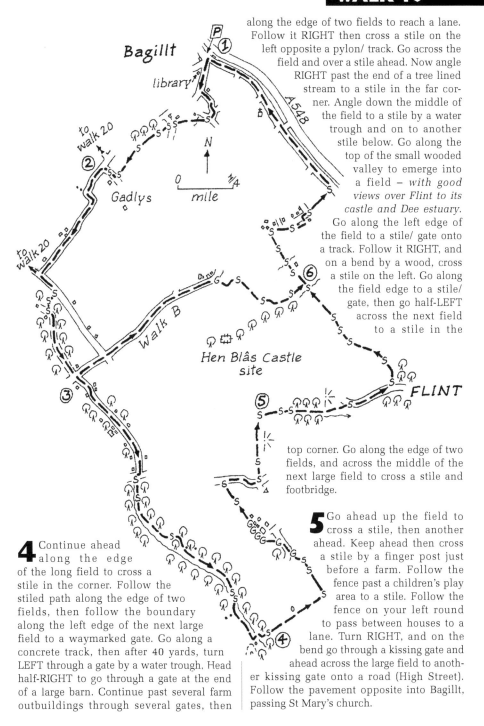

Bagillt

library

to walk 20

Gadlys

② to walk 20

③

N

0   ¼   mile

Walk B

Hen Blâs Castle site

⑤

④

A548

⑥

FLINT

along the edge of two fields to reach a lane. Follow it RIGHT then cross a stile on the left opposite a pylon/ track. Go across the field and over a stile ahead. Now angle RIGHT past the end of a tree lined stream to a stile in the far corner. Angle down the middle of the field to a stile by a water trough and on to another stile below. Go along the top of the small wooded valley to emerge into a field – *with good views over Flint to its castle and Dee estuary.* Go along the left edge of the field to a stile/ gate onto a track. Follow it RIGHT, and on a bend by a wood, cross a stile on the left. Go along the field edge to a stile/ gate, then go half-LEFT across the next field to a stile in the

top corner. Go along the edge of two fields, and across the middle of the next large field to cross a stile and footbridge.

5 Go ahead up the field to cross a stile, then another ahead. Keep ahead then cross a stile by a finger post just before a farm. Follow the fence past a children's play area to a stile. Follow the fence on your left round to pass between houses to a lane. Turn RIGHT, and on the bend go through a kissing gate and ahead across the large field to another kissing gate onto a road (High Street). Follow the pavement opposite into Bagillt, passing St Mary's church.

4 Continue ahead along the edge of the long field to cross a stile in the corner. Follow the stiled path along the edge of two fields, then follow the boundary along the left edge of the next large field to a waymarked gate. Go along a concrete track, then after 40 yards, turn LEFT through a gate by a water trough. Head half-RIGHT to go through a gate at the end of a large barn. Continue past several farm outbuildings through several gates, then

WALK 20

EAST OF HOLYWELL

DESCRIPTION A 4½ mile walk (**A**) from Holywell or a 3¾ mile walk (**B**) from Boot End, exploring the delightful undulating countryside between Holywell and Bagillt, with good views across the Dee estuary. Allow about 3 hours. The route can also be undertaken as two shorter circuits: a 3¾ mile walk (**C**) from Holywell or a 2½ mile walk (**D**) from Boot End using the quiet country link road as shown.

START Holywell [SJ 188758] or near The Boot and Ship, Boot End [SJ 211761].

DIRECTIONS For the alternative start, take the A5026 from Holywell down to The Boot and Ship on the old A548 road. Turn right to find roadside parking. Walk back to The Boot and Ship and follow instructions from paragraph **6**.

I From the bus terminus take the A5026 road signposted to Bagillt (Coleshill Street). Follow the road out of Holywell. Just after the speed derestriction signs, angle down a path on the right and follow a minor road down into a wooded valley. After passing over a stream continue up the road.

2 Shortly take a signposted path through a kissing gate. (For the next mile you are on Wat's Dyke Way.) Go through the trees to briefly join the stream, then bend away to climb a stepped path on the left up the slope. Now follow a good path through the wooded valley above the stream. Shortly, take the path's left fork to where the stream is joined by another, then follow the stepped path up through the trees, soon meandering more steeply to cross a stile into a field corner.

3 Follow the boundary on your left to a stile in the far corner. Continue along the edge of the next field – *enjoying fine views over the Dee estuary to Hilbre island, the Wirral, Liverpool beyond with its distinctive cathedral, and on a clear day up the Lancashire coast* – to cross a stile in the corner. Continue ahead along the field past

nearby old farm buildings to cross a stile in the corner near cottages. Cross another stile ahead by a finger post. Cross the adjoining stile and continue with Wat's Dyke Way alongside the boundary on your left to a stile in the corner. Go across the middle of the next field to cross a stile by a tree. Now go half-RIGHT up the field to join and follow a hedge to a stile/gate in the corner onto a track/road junction, where you meet the signposted National Cycle Trail no. 5.

4 Go ahead up the road, then take a signposted path over a stile on the left opposite a farm entrance. Go down the field edge to a stile/gate in the corner, then go down the next field – *enjoying panoramic views along the Dee estuary* – to cross a stream and stile at the bottom. Continue ahead alongside the hedge/tree boundary – *enjoying new views east to the Dee bridge at Flint, and distant Beeston castle and Peckforton hills in Cheshire.* When the boundary bends left, continue down the large field aiming for the left-hand end of a large green barn to reach a stile/gate in a kink in the boundary at the field bottom. Turn LEFT along the next field edge to cross a stile to the left of the barn. Cross two further stiles to reach a road. Follow it LEFT. At a junction by a house, turn LEFT along Old Bagillt Road.

5 When you reach the back of Ffordd-y-dre, take a signposted path over a stile on the right. (For **Walk C** continue along the road.) Go down the field edge to a stile in the boundary ahead. Continue down the edge of the next field, and in the bottom corner turn RIGHT to go through a gate by a signposted path junction. Continue ahead beside the hedge to go through an open gateway in the corner. *Ahead are close views of the estuary and a cluster of small boats in an inlet. It is difficult to imagine that just below is Bagillt, a major road and the railway.* Go straight ahead down the field to cross two stiles in the bottom boundary. Now go half-RIGHT down the next field to cross a stile in the corner onto a track by a green outbuilding and a house. Turn LEFT and immediately LEFT again along a path between walls. Follow the wall on your right to its end, then turn

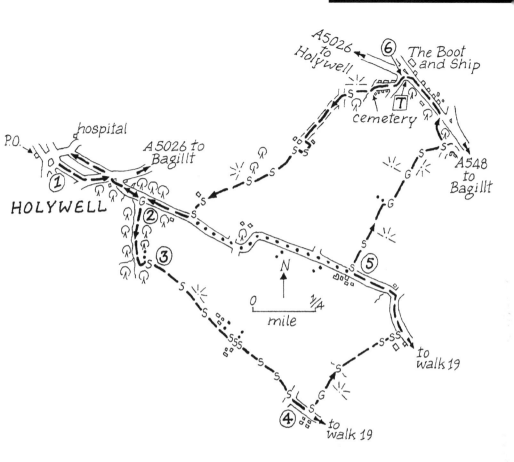

RIGHT down the path to the road near the Bagillt by-pass. Turn LEFT along the pavement.

6 Turn up New Brighton road opposite The Boot and Ship. When it splits go up its RIGHT fork to the cemetery entrance. Just beyond go through a kissing gate and follow the signposted Pennant Walk up the field edge to go through a gap in the corner tree boundary and on through a metal barrier. Turn LEFT up a tree-lined track. At Garreg Lyden – *dating from the 17thC it was once an inn on an ancient road, then a farm* – turn LEFT. Follow the waymarked path down through trees for a few yards,

then bear RIGHT alongside the large fence to cross a stile into a field. Turn RIGHT up the field edge to cross another stile, then turn LEFT and continue alongside the hedge to a stile/gate in the corner. Keep ahead alongside the fence to another stile/gate. Continue along a farm track – *with good views towards Holywell, with the converted 18thC windmill soon becoming visible to the west* – past farm buildings to reach a road. Turn RIGHT. (For **Walk D** follow the road left to point **5**.) After passing Pen yr allt the road descends into the wooded valley to rejoin your outward route. (For **Walk B** go through the kissing gate at point **2**.) At the A5026, take the road opposite (Rose Hill) back into Holywell centre.

PRONUNCIATION

These basic points should help non-Welsh speakers

Welsh	English equivalent
c	always hard, as in cat
ch	as in the Scottish word loch
dd	as th in then
f	as f in of
ff	as ff in off
g	always hard as in got
ll	no real equivalent. It is like 'th' in then, but with an 'L' sound added to it, giving 'thlan' for the pronunciation of the Welsh 'Llan'.

In Welsh the accent usually falls on the last-but-one syllable of a word.

KEY TO THE MAPS

- ➟ Walk route and direction
- ═ Metalled road
- ─ ─ ─ Unsurfaced road
- •••• Footpath/route adjoining walk route
- ⌇ River/stream
- ⚘ ۞ Trees
- ▬■▬ Railway
- **G** Gate
- **S** Stile
- ☀ Viewpoint
- Ⓟ Parking
- Ⓣ Telephone

Useful telephone numbers

Flintshire Highways Department	01352 701233
Flintshire Countryside Service	01244 814931
Flintshire Busline	01352 704035
traveline cymru	0871 200 22 33

THE COUNTRY CODE

- Be safe – plan ahead and follow any signs

- Leave gates and property as you find them

- Protect plants and animals, and take your litter home

- Keep dogs under close control

- Consider other people

Open Access

Open Access land on Halkyn Mountain designated under The CRoW Act 2000 is detailed on the relevant OS map. Access can be subject to restrictions and closure for land management or safety reasons for up to 28 days a year. Please respect any notices. The Countryside Council for Wales website (www.ccw.gov.uk) provides updated information on any closures.

Published by
Kittiwake
3 Glantwymyn Village Workshops,
Glantwymyn, Machynlleth, Montgomeryshire
SY20 8LY
© Text & map research: David Berry 2010
© Maps & illustrations: Kittiwake 2010
Main cover photograph: View from Ffagnallt (Walk 17). *Inset:* Beacon watchtower, near Whitford (Walk 5). *David Berry.*

Printed by MWL, Pontypool
First published 2003. Revised reprint 2006.
Reprinted 2008, 2009. New edition 2010.

ISBN: 978 1 902302 75 1